Contents

Introduction

The International English Language Testing System (IELTS) is widely recognised as a reliable means of assessing the language ability of candidates who need to study or work where English is the language of communication. These Practice Tests are designed to give future IELTS candidates an idea of whether their English is at the required level.

IELTS is owned by three partners, Cambridge English Language Assessment, part of the University of Cambridge, the British Council and IDP Education Pty Limited (through its subsidiary company, IELTS Australia Pty Limited). Further information on IELTS can be found on the IELTS website www.ielts.org.

WHAT IS THE TEST FORMAT?

IELTS consists of four components. All candidates take the same Listening and Speaking tests. There is a choice of Reading and Writing tests according to whether a candidate is taking the Academic or General Training module.

Academic	General Training
For candidates wishing to study at undergraduate or postgraduate levels, and for those seeking professional registration.	For candidates wishing to migrate to an English-speaking country (Australia, Canada, New Zealand, UK), and for those wishing to train or study at below degree level.

The test components are taken in the following order:

Listening		
4 sections, 40 items approximately 30 minutes		
Academic Reading 3 sections, 40 items 60 minutes	or	**General Training Reading** 3 sections, 40 items 60 minutes
Academic Writing 2 tasks 60 minutes	or	**General Training Writing** 2 tasks 60 minutes
Speaking 11 to 14 minutes		
Total Test Time 2 hours 44 minutes		

CAMBR
UNIVERSIT

Z997136

GE ENGLISH
sment
Cambridge

Cambridge English

OFFICIAL

CAMBRIDGE PREPARATION MATERIAL

IELTS 10

WITH ANSWERS

AUTHENTIC EXAMINATION PAPERS FROM CAMBRIDGE ENGLISH LANGUAGE ASSESSMENT

Cambridge University Press
www.cambridge.org/elt

Cambridge English Language Assessment
www.cambridgeenglish.org

Information on this title: www.cambridge.org/9781107464407

© Cambridge University Press and UCLES 2015

First published 2015
8th printing 2016

Printed in Italy by Rotolito Lombarda S.p.A.

A catalogue record for this publication is available from the British Library

ISBN 978-1-107-46440-7 Student's Book with answers
ISBN 978-1-107-46443-8 Student's Book with answers with audio
ISBN 978-1-107-46442-1 Audio CDs (2)

Listening

This test consists of four sections, each with ten questions. The first two sections are concerned with social needs. The first section is a conversation between two speakers and the second section is a monologue. The final two sections are concerned with situations related to educational or training contexts. The third section is a conversation between up to four people and the fourth section is a monologue.

A variety of question types is used, including: multiple choice, matching, plan/map/ diagram labelling, form completion, note completion, table completion, flow-chart completion, summary completion, sentence completion, short-answer questions.

Candidates hear the recording once only and answer the questions as they listen. Ten minutes are allowed at the end for candidates to transfer their answers to the answer sheet.

Academic Reading

This test consists of three sections with 40 questions. There are three texts, which are taken from journals, books, magazines and newspapers. The texts are on topics of general interest. At least one text contains detailed logical argument.

A variety of question types is used, including: multiple choice, identifying information (True/False/Not Given), identifying the writer's views/claims (Yes/No/Not Given), matching information, matching headings, matching features, matching sentence endings, sentence completion, summary completion, note completion, table completion, flow-chart completion, diagram label completion, short-answer questions.

General Training Reading

This test consists of three sections with 40 questions. The texts are taken from notices, advertisements, leaflets, newspapers, instruction manuals, books and magazines. The first section contains texts relevant to basic linguistic survival in English, with tasks mainly concerned with providing factual information. The second section focuses on the work context and involves texts of more complex language. The third section involves reading more extended texts, with a more complex structure, but with the emphasis on descriptive and instructive rather than argumentative texts.

A variety of question types is used, including: multiple choice, identifying information (True/False/Not Given), identifying the writer's views/claims (Yes/No/Not Given), matching information, matching headings, matching features, matching sentence endings, sentence completion, summary completion, note completion, table completion, flow-chart completion, diagram label completion, short-answer questions.

Academic Writing

This test consists of two tasks. It is suggested that candidates spend about 20 minutes on Task 1, which requires them to write at least 150 words, and 40 minutes on Task 2, which requires them to write at least 250 words. Task 2 contributes twice as much as Task 1 to the Writing score.

Task 1 requires candidates to look at a diagram or some data (graph, table or chart) and to present the information in their own words. They are assessed on their ability to organise, present and possibly compare data, describe the stages of a process, describe an object or event, or explain how something works.

In Task 2 candidates are presented with a point of view, argument or problem. They are assessed on their ability to present a solution to the problem, present and justify an opinion, compare and contrast evidence and opinions, evaluate and challenge ideas, evidence or arguments.

Candidates are also assessed on their ability to write in an appropriate style.

General Training Writing

This test consists of two tasks. It is suggested that candidates spend about 20 minutes on Task 1, which requires them to write at least 150 words, and 40 minutes on Task 2, which requires them to write at least 250 words. Task 2 contributes twice as much as Task 1 to the Writing score.

In Task 1 candidates are asked to respond to a given situation with a letter requesting information or explaining the situation. They are assessed on their ability to engage in personal correspondence, elicit and provide general factual information, express needs, wants, likes and dislikes, express opinions, complaints, etc.

In Task 2 candidates are presented with a point of view, argument or problem. They are assessed on their ability to provide general factual information, outline a problem and present a solution, present and justify an opinion, evaluate and challenge ideas, evidence or arguments.

Candidates are also assessed on their ability to write in an appropriate style.

More information on assessing both the Academic and General Training Writing tests, including Writing Assessment Criteria (public version), is available on the IELTS website.

Speaking

This test takes between 11 and 14 minutes and is conducted by a trained examiner. There are three parts:

Part 1

The candidate and the examiner introduce themselves. Candidates then answer general questions about themselves, their home/family, their job/studies, their interests and a wide range of similar familiar topic areas. This part lasts between four and five minutes.

Part 2

The candidate is given a task card with prompts and is asked to talk on a particular topic. The candidate has one minute to prepare and they can make some notes if they wish, before speaking for between one and two minutes. The examiner then asks one or two questions on the same topic.

Part 3

The examiner and the candidate engage in a discussion of more abstract issues which are thematically linked to the topic in Part 2. The discussion lasts between four and five minutes.

The Speaking test assesses whether candidates can communicate effectively in English. The assessment takes into account Fluency and Coherence, Lexical Resource, Grammatical Range and Accuracy, and Pronunciation. More information on assessing the Speaking test, including Speaking Assessment Criteria (public version), is available on the IELTS website.

HOW IS IELTS SCORED?

IELTS results are reported on a nine-band scale. In addition to the score for overall language ability, IELTS provides a score in the form of a profile for each of the four skills (Listening, Reading, Writing and Speaking). These scores are also reported on a nine-band scale. All scores are recorded on the Test Report Form along with details of the candidate's nationality, first language and date of birth. Each Overall Band Score corresponds to a descriptive statement which gives a summary of the English language ability of a candidate classified at that level. The nine bands and their descriptive statements are as follows:

9 **Expert User** – *Has fully operational command of the language: appropriate, accurate and fluent with complete understanding.*

8 **Very Good User** – *Has fully operational command of the language with only occasional unsystematic inaccuracies and inappropriacies. Misunderstandings may occur in unfamiliar situations. Handles complex detailed argumentation well.*

7 **Good User** – *Has operational command of the language, though with occasional inaccuracies, inappropriacies and misunderstandings in some situations. Generally handles complex language well and understands detailed reasoning.*

6 **Competent User** – *Has generally effective command of the language despite some inaccuracies, inappropriacies and misunderstandings. Can use and understand fairly complex language, particularly in familiar situations.*

5 **Modest User** – *Has partial command of the language, coping with overall meaning in most situations, though is likely to make many mistakes. Should be able to handle basic communication in own field.*

4 **Limited User** – *Basic competence is limited to familiar situations. Has frequent problems in understanding and expression. Is not able to use complex language.*

3 **Extremely Limited User** – *Conveys and understands only general meaning in very familiar situations. Frequent breakdowns in communication occur.*

2 **Intermittent User** – *No real communication is possible except for the most basic information using isolated words or short formulae in familiar situations and to meet immediate needs. Has great difficulty understanding spoken and written English.*

1 **Non User** – *Essentially has no ability to use the language beyond possibly a few isolated words.*

0 **Did not attempt the test** – *No assessable information provided.*

Most universities and colleges in the United Kingdom, Australia, New Zealand, Canada and the USA accept an IELTS Overall Band Score of 6.0 – 7.0 for entry to academic programmes.

MARKING THE PRACTICE TESTS

Listening and Reading

The Answer keys are on pages 151–160.
Each question in the Listening and Reading tests is worth one mark.

Questions which require letter / Roman numeral answers

- For questions where the answers are letters or Roman numerals, you should write *only* the number of answers required. For example, if the answer is a single letter or numeral you should write only one answer. If you have written more letters or numerals than are required, the answer must be marked wrong.

Questions which require answers in the form of words or numbers

- Answers may be written in upper or lower case.
- Words in brackets are *optional* – they are correct, but not necessary.
- Alternative answers are separated by a slash (/).
- If you are asked to write an answer using a certain number of words and/or (a) number(s), you will be penalised if you exceed this. For example, if a question specifies an answer using NO MORE THAN THREE WORDS and the correct answer is 'black leather coat', the answer 'coat of black leather' is *incorrect*.
- In questions where you are expected to complete a gap, you should only transfer the necessary missing word(s) onto the answer sheet. For example, to complete 'in the …', and the correct answer is 'morning', the answer 'in the morning' would be *incorrect*.
- All answers require correct spelling (including words in brackets).
- Both US and UK spelling are acceptable and are included in the Answer Key.
- All standard alternatives for numbers, dates and currencies are acceptable.
- All standard abbreviations are acceptable.
- You will find additional notes about individual answers in the Answer Key.

Writing

The model and sample answers are on pages 161–172. It is not possible for you to give yourself a mark for the Writing tasks. For Task 2 in Tests 1 and 3, and Task 1 in Tests 2 and 4, and for Task 1 in General Training Test A and Task 2 in General Training Test B, we have provided model answers (written by an examiner). It is important to note that these show just one way of completing the task, out of many possible approaches. For Task 1 in Tests 1 and 3, and Task 2 in Tests 2 and 4, and for Task 2 in General Training Test A and Task 1 in General Training Test B, we have provided sample answers (written by candidates), showing their score and the examiner's comments. These model answers and sample answers will give you an insight into what is required for the Writing test.

HOW SHOULD YOU INTERPRET YOUR SCORES?

At the end of the each Listening and Reading Answer key you will find a chart which will help you assess whether, on the basis of your Practice Test results, you are ready to take the IELTS test.

In interpreting your score, there are a number of points you should bear in mind. Your performance in the real IELTS test will be reported in two ways: there will be a Band Score from 1 to 9 for each of the components and an Overall Band Score from 1 to 9, which is the average of your scores in the four components. However, institutions considering your application are advised to look at both the Overall Band Score and the Bands for each component in order to determine whether you have the language skills needed for a particular course of study. For example, if your course has a lot of reading and writing, but no lectures, listening skills might be less important and a score of 5 in Listening might be acceptable if the Overall Band Score was 7. However, for a course which has lots of lectures and spoken instructions, a score of 5 in Listening might be unacceptable even though the Overall Band Score was 7.

Once you have marked your tests you should have some idea of whether your listening and reading skills are good enough for you to try the IELTS test. If you did well enough in one component but not in others, you will have to decide for yourself whether you are ready to take the test.

The Practice Tests have been checked to ensure that they are of approximately the same level of difficulty as the real IELTS test. However, we cannot guarantee that your score in the Practice Tests will be reflected in the real IELTS test. The Practice Tests can only give you an idea of your possible future performance and it is ultimately up to you to make decisions based on your score.

Different institutions accept different IELTS scores for different types of courses. We have based our recommendations on the average scores which the majority of institutions accept. The institution to which you are applying may, of course, require a higher or lower score than most other institutions.

Further information

For more information about IELTS or any other Cambridge English Language Assessment examination, write to:

Cambridge English Language Assessment
1 Hills Road
Cambridge
CB1 2EU
United Kingdom

https://support.cambridgeenglish.org
http://www.ielts.org

Test 1

SECTION 1   Questions 1–10

Questions 1–6

Complete the notes below.

*Write **ONE WORD** for each answer.*

SELF-DRIVE TOURS IN THE USA	
Example	
Name:	**Andrea** .... *Brown* ....
Address:	24 **1** .... Road
Postcode:	BH5 2OP
Phone:	(mobile) 077 8664 3091
Heard about company from:	**2** ....
Possible self-drive tours	
Trip One:	
• Los Angeles: customer wants to visit some **3** .... parks with her children	
• Yosemite Park: customer wants to stay in a lodge, not a **4**	
Trip Two:	
• Customer wants to see the **5** .... on the way to Cambria	
• At Santa Monica: not interested in shopping	
• At San Diego, wants to spend time on the **6**	

10

Questions 7–10

Complete the table below.

Write **ONE WORD AND/OR A NUMBER** *for each answer.*

	Number of days	**Total distance**	**Price (per person)**	**Includes**
Trip One	12 days	**7** .... km	£525	• accommodation • car • one **8** ....
Trip Two	9 days	980 km	**9** £	• accommodation • car • **10** ....

SECTION 2   *Questions 11–20*

Questions 11–12

*Choose **TWO** letters **A–E**.*

Which **TWO** facilities at the leisure club have recently been improved?

    A   the gym
    B   the tracks
    C   the indoor pool
    D   the outdoor pool
    E   the sports training for children

Questions 13–20

Complete the notes below.

*Write **NO MORE THAN TWO WORDS** for each answer.*

Joining the leisure club

Personal Assessment

*   New members should describe any **13** ....
*   The **14** .... will be explained to you before you use the equipment.
*   You will be given a six-week **15** ....

Types of membership

*   There is a compulsory £90 **16** .... fee for members.
*   Gold members are given **17** .... to all the LP clubs.
*   Premier members are given priority during **18** .... hours.
*   Premier members can bring some **19** .... every month.
*   Members should always take their **20** .... with them.

SECTION 3   *Questions 21–30*

Questions 21–25

Choose the correct letter, **A**, **B** *or* **C**.

Global Design Competition

21 Students entering the design competition have to

    A   produce an energy-efficient design.
    B   adapt an existing energy-saving appliance.
    C   develop a new use for current technology.

22 John chose a dishwasher because he wanted to make dishwashers

    A   more appealing.
    B   more common.
    C   more economical.

23 The stone in John's 'Rockpool' design is used

    A   for decoration.
    B   to switch it on.
    C   to stop water escaping.

24 In the holding chamber, the carbon dioxide

    A   changes back to a gas.
    B   dries the dishes.
    C   is allowed to cool.

25 At the end of the cleaning process, the carbon dioxide

    A   is released into the air.
    B   is disposed of with the waste.
    C   is collected ready to be re-used.

Questions 26–30

Complete the notes below.

*Write **ONE WORD ONLY** for each answer.*

- John needs help preparing for his **26** ....

- The professor advises John to make a **27** .... of his design.

- John's main problem is getting good quality **28** ....

- The professor suggests John apply for a **29** ....

- The professor will check the **30** .... information in John's written report.

SECTION 4 *Questions 31–40*

Complete the notes below.

Write ONE WORD ONLY for each answer.

THE SPIRIT BEAR

General facts

- It is a white bear belonging to the black bear family.
- Its colour comes from an uncommon **31** ....
- Local people believe that it has unusual **32** ....
- They protect the bear from **33** ....

Habitat

- The bear's relationship with the forest is complex.
- Tree roots stop **34** .... along salmon streams.
- The bears' feeding habits provide nutrients for forest vegetation.
- It is currently found on a small number of **35** ....

Threats

- Habitat is being lost due to deforestation and construction of **36** .... by logging companies.
- Unrestricted **37** .... is affecting the salmon supply.
- The bears' existence is also threatened by their low rate of **38** ....

Going forward

- Interested parties are working together.
- Logging companies must improve their **39** .... of logging.
- Maintenance and **40** .... of the spirit bears' territory is needed.

READING

READING PASSAGE 1

*You should spend about 20 minutes on **Questions 1–13**, which are based on Reading Passage 1 below.*

Stepwells

A millennium ago, stepwells were fundamental to life in the driest parts of India. Richard Cox travelled to north-western India to document these spectacular monuments from a bygone era

During the sixth and seventh centuries, the inhabitants of the modern-day states of Gujarat and Rajasthan in north-western India developed a method of gaining access to clean, fresh groundwater during the dry season for drinking, bathing, watering animals and irrigation. However, the significance of this invention – the stepwell – goes beyond its utilitarian application.

Unique to this region, stepwells are often architecturally complex and vary widely in size and shape. During their heyday, they were places of gathering, of leisure and relaxation and of worship for villagers of all but the lowest classes. Most stepwells are found dotted round the desert areas of Gujarat (where they are called *vav*) and Rajasthan (where they are called *baori),* while a few also survive in Delhi. Some were located in or near villages as public spaces for the community; others were positioned beside roads as resting places for travellers.

As their name suggests, stepwells comprise a series of stone steps descending from ground level to the water source (normally an underground aquifer) as it recedes following the rains. When the water level was high, the user needed only to descend a few steps to reach it; when it was low, several levels would have to be negotiated.

Some wells are vast, open craters with hundreds of steps paving each sloping side, often in tiers. Others are more elaborate, with long stepped passages leading to the water via several storeys. Built from stone and supported by pillars, they also included pavilions that sheltered visitors from the relentless heat. But perhaps the most impressive features are the intricate decorative sculptures that embellish many stepwells, showing activities from fighting and dancing to everyday acts such as women combing their hair or churning butter.

Down the centuries, thousands of wells were constructed throughout north-western India, but the majority have now fallen into disuse; many are derelict and dry, as groundwater has been diverted for industrial use and the wells no longer reach the water table. Their condition hasn't been helped by recent dry spells: southern Rajasthan suffered an eight-year drought between 1996 and 2004.

However, some important sites in Gujarat have recently undergone major restoration, and the state government announced in June last year that it plans to restore the stepwells throughout the state.

In Patan, the state's ancient capital, the stepwell of *Rani Ki Vav* (Queen's Stepwell) is perhaps the finest current example. It was built by Queen Udayamati during the late 11th century, but became silted up following a flood during the 13th century. But the Archaeological Survey of India began restoring it in the 1960s, and today it is in pristine condition. At 65 metres long, 20 metres wide and 27 metres deep, *Rani Ki Vav* features 500 sculptures carved into niches throughout the monument. Incredibly, in January 2001, this ancient structure survived an earthquake that measured 7.6 on the Richter scale.

Another example is the *Surya Kund* in Modhera, northern Gujarat, next to the Sun Temple, built by King Bhima I in 1026 to honour the sun god Surya. It actually resembles a tank (*kund* means reservoir or pond) rather than a well, but displays the hallmarks of stepwell architecture, including four sides of steps that descend to the bottom in a stunning geometrical formation. The terraces house 108 small, intricately carved shrines between the sets of steps.

Rajasthan also has a wealth of wells. The ancient city of Bundi, 200 kilometres south of Jaipur, is renowned for its architecture, including its stepwells.

One of the larger examples is *Raniji Ki Baori*, which was built by the queen of the region, Nathavatji, in 1699. At 46 metres deep, 20 metres wide and 40 metres long, the intricately carved monument is one of 21 *baoris* commissioned in the Bundi area by Nathavatji.

In the old ruined town of Abhaneri, about 95 kilometres east of Jaipur, is *Chand Baori*, one of India's oldest and deepest wells; aesthetically it's perhaps one of the most dramatic. Built in around 850 AD next to the temple of Harshat Mata, the *baori* comprises hundreds of zigzagging steps that run along three of its sides, steeply descending 11 storeys, resulting in a striking pattern when seen from afar. On the fourth side, verandas which are supported by ornate pillars overlook the steps.

Still in public use is *Neemrana Ki Baori*, located just off the Jaipur–Delhi highway. Constructed in around 1700, it is nine storeys deep, with the last two being underwater. At ground level, there are 86 colonnaded openings from where the visitor descends 170 steps to the deepest water source.

Today, following years of neglect, many of these monuments to medieval engineering have been saved by the Archaeological Survey of India, which has recognised the importance of preserving them as part of the country's rich history. Tourists flock to wells in far-flung corners of north-western India to gaze in wonder at these architectural marvels from hundreds of years ago, which serve as a reminder of both the ingenuity and artistry of ancient civilisations and of the value of water to human existence.

Questions 1–5

Do the following statements agree with the information given in Reading Passage 1?

In boxes 1–5 on your answer sheet, write

> **TRUE**   *if the statement agrees with the information*
> **FALSE**   *if the statement contradicts the information*
> **NOT GIVEN** *if there is no information on this*

1   Examples of ancient stepwells can be found all over the world.

2   Stepwells had a range of functions, in addition to those related to water collection.

3   The few existing stepwells in Delhi are more attractive than those found elsewhere.

4   It took workers many years to build the stone steps characteristic of stepwells.

5   The number of steps above the water level in a stepwell altered during the course of a year.

Questions 6–8

Answer the questions below.

*Choose **ONE WORD ONLY** from the passage for each answer.*

Write your answers in boxes 6–8 on your answer sheet.

6   Which part of some stepwells provided shade for people?

7   What type of serious climatic event, which took place in southern Rajasthan, is mentioned in the article?

8   Who are frequent visitors to stepwells nowadays?

Test 1

Questions 9–13

Complete the table below.

Choose **ONE WORD AND/OR A NUMBER** *from the passage for each answer.*

Write your answers in boxes 9–13 on your answer sheet.

Stepwell	Date	Features	Other notes
Rani Ki Vav	Late 11th century	As many as 500 sculptures decorate the monument	Restored in the 1960s Excellent condition, despite the **9** .... of 2001
Surya Kund	1026	Steps on the **10** .... produce a geometrical pattern Carved shrines	Looks more like a **11** .... than a well
Raniji Ki Baori	1699	Intricately carved monument	One of 21 *baoris* in the area commissioned by Queen Nathavatji
Chand Baori	850 AD	Steps take you down 11 storeys to the bottom	Old, deep and very dramatic Has **12** .... which provide a view of the steps
Neemrana Ki Baori	1700	Has two **13** .... levels	Used by public today

READING PASSAGE 2

*You should spend about 20 minutes on **Questions 14–26**, which are based on Reading Passage 2 on the following pages.*

Questions 14–21

Reading Passage 2 has nine paragraphs, **A–I**.

*Choose the correct heading for paragraphs **A–E** and **G–I** from the list of headings below.*

*Write the correct number, **i–xi**, in boxes 14–21 on your answer sheet.*

List of Headings
i   A fresh and important long-term goal
ii   Charging for roads and improving other transport methods
iii   Changes affecting the distances goods may be transported
iv   Taking all the steps necessary to change transport patterns
v   The environmental costs of road transport
vi   The escalating cost of rail transport
vii   The need to achieve transport rebalance
viii The rapid growth of private transport
ix   Plans to develop major road networks
x   Restricting road use through charging policies alone
xi   Transport trends in countries awaiting EU admission

14   Paragraph **A**   19   Paragraph **G**

15   Paragraph **B**   20   Paragraph **H**

16   Paragraph **C**   21   Paragraph **I**

17   Paragraph **D**

18   Paragraph **E**

Example	*Answer*
Paragraph **F**	**vii**

EUROPEAN TRANSPORT SYSTEMS 1990-2010

What have been the trends and what are the prospects for European transport systems?

A It is difficult to conceive of vigorous economic growth without an efficient transport system. Although modern information technologies can reduce the demand for physical transport by facilitating teleworking and teleservices, the requirement for transport continues to increase. There are two key factors behind this trend. For passenger transport, the determining factor is the spectacular growth in car use. The number of cars on European Union (EU) roads saw an increase of three million cars each year from 1990 to 2010, and in the next decade the EU will see a further substantial increase in its fleet.

B As far as goods transport is concerned, growth is due to a large extent to changes in the European economy and its system of production. In the last 20 years, as internal frontiers have been abolished, the EU has moved from a 'stock' economy to a 'flow' economy. This phenomenon has been emphasised by the relocation of some industries, particularly those which are labour intensive, to reduce production costs, even though the production site is hundreds or even thousands of kilometres away from the final assembly plant or away from users.

C The strong economic growth expected in countries which are candidates for entry to the EU will also increase transport flows, in particular road haulage traffic. In 1998, some of these countries already exported more than twice their 1990 volumes and imported more than five times their 1990 volumes. And although many candidate countries inherited a transport system which encourages rail, the distribution between modes has tipped sharply in favour of road transport since the 1990s. Between 1990 and 1998, road haulage increased by 19.4%, while during the same period rail haulage decreased by 43.5%, although – and this could benefit the enlarged EU – it is still on average at a much higher level than in existing member states.

D However, a new imperative – sustainable development – offers an opportunity for adapting the EU's common transport policy. This objective, agreed by the Gothenburg European Council, has to be achieved by integrating environmental considerations into Community policies, and shifting the balance between modes of transport lies at the heart of its strategy. The ambitious objective can only be fully achieved by 2020, but proposed measures are nonetheless a first essential step towards a sustainable transport system which will ideally be in place in 30 years' time, that is by 2040.

E In 1998, energy consumption in the transport sector was to blame for 28% of emissions of CO_2, the leading greenhouse gas. According to the latest estimates, if nothing is done to reverse the traffic growth trend, CO_2 emissions from transport can be expected to increase by around 50% to 1,113 billion tonnes by 2020, compared with the 739 billion tonnes recorded in 1990. Once again, road transport is the main culprit since it alone accounts for 84% of the CO_2 emissions attributable to transport. Using alternative fuels and improving energy efficiency is thus both an ecological necessity and a technological challenge.

F At the same time greater efforts must be made to achieve a modal shift. Such a change cannot be achieved overnight, all the less so after over half a century of constant deterioration in favour of road. This has reached such a pitch that today rail freight services are facing marginalisation, with just 8% of market share, and with international goods trains struggling along at an average speed of 18km/h. Three possible options have emerged.

G The first approach would consist of focusing on road transport solely through pricing. This option would not be accompanied by complementary measures in the other modes of transport. In the short term it might curb the growth in road transport through the better loading ratio of goods vehicles and occupancy rates of passenger vehicles expected as a result of the increase in the price of transport. However, the lack of measures available to revitalise other modes of transport would make it impossible for more sustainable modes of transport to take up the baton.

H The second approach also concentrates on road transport pricing but is accompanied by measures to increase the efficiency of the other modes (better quality of services, logistics, technology). However, this approach does not include investment in new infrastructure, nor does it guarantee better regional cohesion. It could help to achieve greater uncoupling than the first approach, but road transport would keep the lion's share of the market and continue to concentrate on saturated arteries, despite being the most polluting of the modes. It is therefore not enough to guarantee the necessary shift of the balance.

I The third approach, which is not new, comprises a series of measures ranging from pricing to revitalising alternative modes of transport and targeting investment in the trans-European network. This integrated approach would allow the market shares of the other modes to return to their 1998 levels and thus make a shift of balance. It is far more ambitious than it looks, bearing in mind the historical imbalance in favour of roads for the last fifty years, but would achieve a marked break in the link between road transport growth and economic growth, without placing restrictions on the mobility of people and goods.

Questions 22–26

Do the following statements agree with the information given in Reading Passage 2?

In boxes 22–26 on your answer sheet, write

TRUE   *if the statement agrees with the information*
FALSE   *if the statement contradicts the information*
NOT GIVEN *if there is no information on this*

22 The need for transport is growing, despite technological developments.

23 To reduce production costs, some industries have been moved closer to their relevant consumers.

24 Cars are prohibitively expensive in some EU candidate countries.

25 The Gothenburg European Council was set up 30 years ago.

26 By the end of this decade, CO_2 emissions from transport are predicted to reach 739 billion tonnes.

READING PASSAGE 3

*You should spend about 20 minutes on **Questions 27–40**, which are based on Reading Passage 3 below.*

The psychology of innovation

Why are so few companies truly innovative?

Innovation is key to business survival, and companies put substantial resources into inspiring employees to develop new ideas. There are, nevertheless, people working in luxurious, state-of-the-art centres designed to stimulate innovation who find that their environment doesn't make them feel at all creative. And there are those who don't have a budget, or much space, but who innovate successfully.

For Robert B. Cialdini, Professor of Psychology at Arizona State University, one reason that companies don't succeed as often as they should is that innovation starts with recruitment. Research shows that the fit between an employee's values and a company's values makes a difference to what contribution they make and whether, two years after they join, they're still at the company. Studies at Harvard Business School show that, although some individuals may be more creative than others, almost every individual can be creative in the right circumstances.

One of the most famous photographs in the story of rock'n'roll emphasises Cialdini's views. The 1956 picture of singers Elvis Presley, Carl Perkins, Johnny Cash and Jerry Lee Lewis jamming at a piano in Sun Studios in Memphis tells a hidden story. Sun's 'million-dollar quartet' could have been a quintet. Missing from the picture is Roy Orbison, a greater natural singer than Lewis, Perkins or Cash. Sam Phillips,

who owned Sun, wanted to revolutionise popular music with songs that fused black and white music, and country and blues. Presley, Cash, Perkins and Lewis instinctively understood Phillips's ambition and believed in it. Orbison wasn't inspired by the goal, and only ever achieved one hit with the Sun label.

The value fit matters, says Cialdini, because innovation is, in part, a process of change, and under that pressure we, as a species, behave differently, 'When things change, we are hard-wired to play it safe.' Managers should therefore adopt an approach that appears counter-intuitive – they should explain what stands to be lost if the company fails to seize a particular opportunity. Studies show that we invariably take more gambles when threatened with a loss than when offered a reward.

Managing innovation is a delicate art. It's easy for a company to be pulled in conflicting directions as the marketing, product development, and finance departments each get different feedback from different sets of people. And without a system which ensures collaborative exchanges within the company, it's also easy for small 'pockets of innovation' to disappear. Innovation is a contact sport. You can't brief people just by saying, 'We're going in this direction and I'm going to take you with me.'

Cialdini believes that this 'follow-the-leader syndrome' is dangerous, not least because it encourages bosses to go it alone. 'It's been scientifically proven that three people will be better than one at solving problems, even if that one person is the smartest person in the field.' To prove his point, Cialdini cites an interview with molecular biologist James Watson. Watson, together with Francis Crick, discovered the structure of DNA, the genetic information carrier of all living organisms. 'When asked how they had cracked the code ahead of an array of highly accomplished rival investigators, he said something that stunned me. He said he and Crick had succeeded because they were aware that they weren't the most intelligent of the scientists pursuing the answer. The smartest scientist was called Rosalind Franklin who, Watson said, "was so intelligent she rarely sought advice".'

Teamwork taps into one of the basic drivers of human behaviour. 'The principle of social proof is so pervasive that we don't even recognise it,' says Cialdini. 'If your project is being resisted, for example, by a group of veteran employees, ask another old-timer to speak up for it.' Cialdini is not alone in advocating this strategy. Research shows that peer power, used horizontally not vertically, is much more powerful than any boss's speech.

Writing, visualising and prototyping can stimulate the flow of new ideas. Cialdini cites scores of research papers and historical events that prove that even something as simple as writing deepens every individual's engagement in the project. It is, he says, the reason why all those competitions on breakfast cereal packets encouraged us to write in saying, in no more than 10 words: 'I like Kellogg's Corn Flakes because… .' The very act of writing makes us more likely to believe it.

Authority doesn't have to inhibit innovation but it often does. The wrong kind of leadership will lead to what Cialdini calls 'captainitis, the regrettable tendency of team members to opt out of team responsibilities that are properly theirs'. He calls it captainitis because, he says, 'crew members of multipilot aircraft exhibit a sometimes deadly passivity when the flight captain makes a clearly wrong-headed decision'. This behaviour is not, he says, unique to air travel, but can happen in any workplace where the leader is overbearing.

At the other end of the scale is the 1980s Memphis design collective, a group of young designers for whom 'the only rule was that there were no rules'. This environment encouraged a free interchange of ideas, which led to more creativity with form, function, colour and materials that revolutionised attitudes to furniture design.

Many theorists believe the ideal boss should lead from behind, taking pride in collective accomplishment and giving credit where it is due. Cialdini says: 'Leaders should encourage everyone to contribute and simultaneously assure all concerned that every recommendation is important to making the right decision and will be given full attention.' The frustrating thing about innovation is that there are many approaches, but no magic formula. However, a manager who wants to create a truly innovative culture can make their job a lot easier by recognising these psychological realities.

Questions 27–30

*Choose the correct letter, **A**, **B**, **C** or **D**.*

Write the correct letter in boxes 27–30 on your answer sheet.

27 The example of the 'million-dollar quartet' underlines the writer's point about

    A   recognising talent.
    B   working as a team.
    C   having a shared objective.
    D   being an effective leader.

28 James Watson suggests that he and Francis Crick won the race to discover the DNA code because they

    A   were conscious of their own limitations.
    B   brought complementary skills to their partnership.
    C   were determined to outperform their brighter rivals.
    D   encouraged each other to realise their joint ambition.

29 The writer mentions competitions on breakfast cereal packets as an example of how to

    A   inspire creative thinking.
    B   generate concise writing.
    C   promote loyalty to a group.
    D   strengthen commitment to an idea.

30 In the last paragraph, the writer suggests that it is important for employees to

    A   be aware of their company's goals.
    B   feel that their contributions are valued.
    C   have respect for their co-workers' achievements.
    D   understand why certain management decisions are made.

Questions 31–35

*Complete each sentence with the correct ending, **A–G**, below.*

*Write the correct letter, **A–G**, in boxes 31–35 on your answer sheet.*

31 Employees whose values match those of their employers are more likely to

32 At times of change, people tend to

33 If people are aware of what they might lose, they will often

34 People working under a dominant boss are liable to

35 Employees working in organisations with few rules are more likely to

A	take chances.
B	share their ideas.
C	become competitive.
D	get promotion.
E	avoid risk.
F	ignore their duties.
G	remain in their jobs.

Questions 36–40

Do the following statements agree with the claims of the writer in Reading Passage 3?

In boxes 36–40 on your answer sheet, write

> **YES**   *if the statement agrees with the claims of the writer*
> **NO**   *if the statement contradicts the claims of the writer*
> **NOT GIVEN**   *if it is impossible to say what the writer thinks about this*

36 The physical surroundings in which a person works play a key role in determining their creativity.

37 Most people have the potential to be creative.

38 Teams work best when their members are of equally matched intelligence.

39 It is easier for smaller companies to be innovative.

40 A manager's approval of an idea is more persuasive than that of a colleague.

WRITING

WRITING TASK 1

You should spend about 20 minutes on this task.

> *The first chart below shows how energy is used in an average Australian household. The second chart shows the greenhouse gas emissions which result from this energy use.*
>
> *Summarise the information by selecting and reporting the main features, and make comparisons where relevant.*

Write at least 150 words.

Australian household energy use

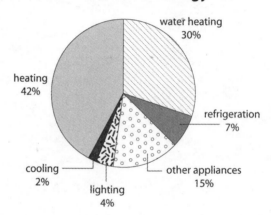

Australian household greenhouse gas emissions

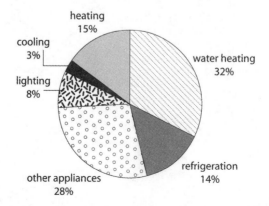

WRITING TASK 2

You should spend about 40 minutes on this task.

Present a written argument or case to an educated reader with no specialist knowledge of the following topic.

> *It is important for children to learn the difference between right and wrong at an early age. Punishment is necessary to help them learn this distinction.*
>
> *To what extent do you agree or disagree with this opinion?*
>
> *What sort of punishment should parents and teachers be allowed to use to teach good behaviour to children?*

Give reasons for your answer and include any relevant examples from your own knowledge or experience.

Write at least 250 words.

SPEAKING

PART 1

The examiner asks the candidate about him/herself, his/her home, work or studies and other familiar topics.

EXAMPLE

Weekends

- How do you usually spend your weekends? [Why?]
- Which is your favourite part of the weekend? [Why?]
- Do you think your weekends are long enough? [Why/Why not?]
- How important do you think it is to have free time at the weekends? [Why?]

PART 2

> **Describe someone you know who does something well.**
>
> **You should say:**
> **who this person is**
> **how you know this person**
> **what they do well**
> **and explain why you think this person is so good at doing this.**

You will have to talk about the topic for one to two minutes.
You have one minute to think about what you are going to say.
You can make some notes to help you if you wish.

PART 3

Discussion topics:

Skills and abilities

Example questions:
What skills and abilities do people most want to have today? Why?
Which skills should children learn at school? Are there any skills which they should learn at home? What are they?
Which skills do you think will be important in the future? Why?

Salaries for skilled people

Example questions:
Which kinds of jobs have the highest salaries in your country? Why is this?
Are there any other jobs that you think should have high salaries? Why do you think that?
Some people say it would be better for society if everyone got the same salary. What do you think about that? Why?

Test 2

LISTENING

SECTION 1   *Questions 1–10*

Complete the notes below.

*Write **ONE WORD AND/OR A NUMBER** for each answer.*

Transport Survey

Example

Travelled to town today: by ....bus..............

Name: Luisa **1** ....

Address: 2 .... White Stone Rd

Area: Bradfield

Postcode: 3 ....

Occupation: 4 ....

Reason for visit to town: to go to the **5** ....

Suggestions for improvement:

*   better **6** ....

*   have more footpaths

*   more frequent **7** ....

Things that would encourage cycling to work:

- having **8** .... parking places for bicycles

- being able to use a **9** .... at work

- the opportunity to have cycling **10** .... on busy roads

SECTION 2   *Questions 11–20*

Questions 11–14

*Choose the correct letter, **A**, **B** or **C**.*

New city developments

11   The idea for the two new developments in the city came from

    A   local people.
    B   the City Council.
    C   the SWRDC.

12   What is unusual about Brackenside pool?

    A   its architectural style
    B   its heating system
    C   its method of water treatment

13   Local newspapers have raised worries about

    A   the late opening date.
    B   the cost of the project.
    C   the size of the facilities.

14   What decision has not yet been made about the pool?

    A   whose statue will be at the door
    B   the exact opening times
    C   who will open it

Questions 15–20

Which feature is related to each of the following areas of the world represented in the playground?

*Choose **SIX** answers from the box and write the correct letter, **A–I**, next to questions 15–20.*

Features
A ancient forts
B waterways
C ice and snow
D jewels
E local animals
F mountains
G music and film
H space travel
I volcanoes

Areas of the world

15 Asia   ....

16 Antarctica   ....

17 South America   ....

18 North America   ....

19 Europe   ....

20 Africa   ....

SECTION 3   *Questions 21–30*

Questions 21 and 22

*Choose **TWO** letters, **A–E**.*

Which **TWO** hobbies was Thor Heyerdahl very interested in as a youth?

    A   camping
    B   climbing
    C   collecting
    D   hunting
    E   reading

Questions 23 and 24

*Choose **TWO** letters, **A–E**.*

Which do the speakers say are the **TWO** reasons why Heyerdahl went to live on an island?

    A   to examine ancient carvings
    B   to experience an isolated place
    C   to formulate a new theory
    D   to learn survival skills
    E   to study the impact of an extreme environment

Questions 25–30

*Choose the correct letter, **A**, **B** or **C**.*

The later life of Thor Heyerdahl

25 According to Victor and Olivia, academics thought that Polynesian migration from the east was impossible due to

  A the fact that Eastern countries were far away.
  B the lack of materials for boat building.
  C the direction of the winds and currents.

26 Which do the speakers agree was the main reason for Heyerdahl's raft journey?

  A to overcome a research setback
  B to demonstrate a personal quality
  C to test a new theory

27 What was most important to Heyerdahl about his raft journey?

  A the fact that he was the first person to do it
  B the speed of crossing the Pacific
  C the use of authentic construction methods

28 Why did Heyerdahl go to Easter Island?

  A to build a stone statue
  B to sail a reed boat
  C to learn the local language

29 In Olivia's opinion, Heyerdahl's greatest influence was on

  A theories about Polynesian origins.
  B the development of archaeological methodology.
  C establishing archaeology as an academic subject.

30 Which criticism do the speakers make of William Oliver's textbook?

  A Its style is out of date.
  B Its content is over-simplified.
  C Its methodology is flawed.

SECTION 4   *Questions 31–40*

Complete the notes below.

Write ONE WORD ONLY for each answer.

THE FUTURE OF MANAGEMENT

Business markets

*   greater **31** .... among companies

*   increase in power of large **32** .... companies

*   rising **33** .... in certain countries

External influences on businesses

*   more discussion with **34** .... before making business decisions

*   environmental concerns which may lead to more **35** ....

Business structures

*   more teams will be formed to work on a particular **36** ....

*   businesses may need to offer hours that are **37** .... , or the chance to work remotely

Management styles

*   increasing need for managers to provide good **38** ....

*   changes influenced by **39** .... taking senior roles

Changes in the economy

- service sector continues to be important

- increasing value of intellectual property

- more and more **40** .... workers

READING PASSAGE 1

*You should spend about 20 minutes on **Questions 1–13**, which are based on Reading Passage 1 on the following pages.*

Questions 1–7

Reading Passage 1 has seven paragraphs, **A–G**.

Choose the correct heading for each paragraph from the list of headings below.

*Write the correct number, **i–ix**, in boxes 1–7 on your answer sheet.*

List of Headings

i	The search for the reasons for an increase in population
ii	Industrialisation and the fear of unemployment
iii	The development of cities in Japan
iv	The time and place of the Industrial Revolution
v	The cases of Holland, France and China
vi	Changes in drinking habits in Britain
vii	Two keys to Britain's industrial revolution
viii	Conditions required for industrialisation
ix	Comparisons with Japan lead to the answer

---

1   Paragraph **A**

2   Paragraph **B**

3   Paragraph **C**

4   Paragraph **D**

5   Paragraph **E**

6   Paragraph **F**

7   Paragraph **G**

Tea and the Industrial Revolution

A Cambridge professor says that a change in drinking habits was the reason for the Industrial Revolution in Britain. Anjana Ahuja reports

A   Alan Macfarlane, professor of anthropological science at King's College, Cambridge, has, like other historians, spent decades wrestling with the enigma of the Industrial Revolution. Why did this particular Big Bang – the world-changing birth of industry – happen in Britain? And why did it strike at the end of the 18th century?

B   Macfarlane compares the puzzle to a combination lock. 'There are about 20 different factors and all of them need to be present before the revolution can happen,' he says. For industry to take off, there needs to be the technology and power to drive factories, large urban populations to provide cheap labour, easy transport to move goods around, an affluent middle-class willing to buy mass-produced objects, a market-driven economy and a political system that allows this to happen. While this was the case for England, other nations, such as Japan, the Netherlands and France also met some of these criteria but were not industrialising. 'All these factors must have been necessary but not sufficient to cause the revolution,' says Macfarlane. 'After all, Holland had everything except coal, while China also had many of these factors. Most historians are convinced there are one or two missing factors that you need to open the lock.'

C   The missing factors, he proposes, are to be found in almost every kitchen cupboard. Tea and beer, two of the nation's favourite drinks, fuelled the revolution. The antiseptic properties of tannin, the active ingredient in tea, and of hops in beer – plus the fact that both are made with boiled water – allowed urban communities to flourish at close quarters without succumbing to water-borne diseases such as dysentery. The theory sounds eccentric but once he starts to explain the detective work that went into his deduction, the scepticism gives way to wary admiration. Macfarlane's case has been strengthened by support from notable quarters – Roy Porter, the distinguished medical historian, recently wrote a favourable appraisal of his research.

D   Macfarlane had wondered for a long time how the Industrial Revolution came about. Historians had alighted on one interesting factor around the mid-18th century that required explanation. Between about 1650 and 1740, the population in Britain was static. But then there was a burst in population growth. Macfarlane says: 'The infant mortality rate halved in the space of 20 years, and this happened in both rural areas and cities, and across all classes. People suggested four possible causes. Was there a sudden change in the viruses and bacteria around? Unlikely. Was there a revolution in medical science? But this was a century before Lister's revolution*. Was there a change in environmental conditions? There were improvements in agriculture that wiped out malaria, but these were small gains. Sanitation did not become widespread until the 19th century. The only option left is food. But the height and weight statistics show a decline. So the food must have got worse. Efforts to explain this sudden reduction in child deaths appeared to draw a blank.'

---

* Joseph Lister was the first doctor to use antiseptic techniques during surgical operations to prevent infections.

E   This population burst seemed to happen at just the right time to provide labour for the Industrial Revolution. 'When you start moving towards an industrial revolution, it is economically efficient to have people living close together,' says Macfarlane. 'But then you get disease, particularly from human waste.' Some digging around in historical records revealed that there was a change in the incidence of water-borne disease at that time, especially dysentery. Macfarlane deduced that whatever the British were drinking must have been important in regulating disease. He says, 'We drank beer. For a long time, the English were protected by the strong antibacterial agent in hops, which were added to help preserve the beer. But in the late 17th century a tax was introduced on malt, the basic ingredient of beer. The poor turned to water and gin and in the 1720s the mortality rate began to rise again. Then it suddenly dropped again. What caused this?'

F   Macfarlane looked to Japan, which was also developing large cities about the same time, and also had no sanitation. Water-borne diseases had a much looser grip on the Japanese population than those in Britain. Could it be the prevalence of tea in their culture? Macfarlane then noted that the history of tea in Britain provided an extraordinary coincidence of dates. Tea was relatively expensive until Britain started a direct clipper trade with China in the early 18th century. By the 1740s, about the time that infant mortality was dipping, the drink was common. Macfarlane guessed that the fact that water had to be boiled, together with the stomach-purifying properties of tea meant that the breast milk provided by mothers was healthier than it had ever been. No other European nation sipped tea like the British, which, by Macfarlane's logic, pushed these other countries out of contention for the revolution.

G   But, if tea is a factor in the combination lock, why didn't Japan forge ahead in a tea-soaked industrial revolution of its own? Macfarlane notes that even though 17th-century Japan had large cities, high literacy rates, even a futures market, it had turned its back on the essence of any work-based revolution by giving up labour-saving devices such as animals, afraid that they would put people out of work. So, the nation that we now think of as one of the most technologically advanced entered the 19th century having 'abandoned the wheel'.

Questions 8–13

Do the following statements agree with the information given in Reading Passage 1?

In boxes 8–13 on your answer sheet, write

TRUE	*if the statement agrees with the information*
FALSE	*if the statement contradicts the information*
NOT GIVEN	*if there is no information on this*

8 China's transport system was not suitable for industry in the 18th century.

9 Tea and beer both helped to prevent dysentery in Britain.

10 Roy Porter disagrees with Professor Macfarlane's findings.

11 After 1740, there was a reduction in population in Britain.

12 People in Britain used to make beer at home.

13 The tax on malt indirectly caused a rise in the death rate.

READING PASSAGE 2

*You should spend about 20 minutes on **Questions 14–26**, which are based on Reading Passage 2 below.*

Gifted children and learning

A Internationally, 'giftedness' is most frequently determined by a score on a general intelligence test, known as an IQ test, which is above a chosen cut-off point, usually at around the top 2–5%. Children's educational environment contributes to the IQ score and the way intelligence is used. For example, a very close positive relationship was found when children's IQ scores were compared with their home educational provision (Freeman, 2010). The higher the children's IQ scores, especially over IQ 130, the better the quality of their educational backup, measured in terms of reported verbal interactions with parents, number of books and activities in their home etc. Because IQ tests are decidedly influenced by what the child has learned, they are to some extent measures of current achievement based on age-norms; that is, how well the children have learned to manipulate their knowledge and know-how within the terms of the test. The vocabulary aspect, for example, is dependent on having heard those words. But IQ tests can neither identify the processes of learning and thinking nor predict creativity.

B Excellence does not emerge without appropriate help. To reach an exceptionally high standard in any area very able children need the means to learn, which includes material to work with and focused challenging tuition – and the encouragement to follow their dream. There appears to be a qualitative difference in the way the intellectually highly able think, compared with more average-ability or older pupils, for whom external regulation by the teacher often compensates for lack of internal regulation. To be at their most effective in their self-regulation, all children can be helped to identify their own ways of learning – metacognition – which will include strategies of planning, monitoring, evaluation, and choice of what to learn. Emotional awareness is also part of metacognition, so children should be helped to be aware of their feelings around the area to be learned, feelings of curiosity or confidence, for example.

C High achievers have been found to use self-regulatory learning strategies more often and more effectively than lower achievers, and are better able to transfer these strategies to deal with unfamiliar tasks. This happens to such a high degree in some children that they appear to be demonstrating talent in particular areas. Overviewing research on the thinking process of highly able children, (Shore and Kanevsky, 1993) put the instructor's problem succinctly: 'If they [the gifted] merely think more quickly, then we need only teach more quickly. If they merely make fewer errors, then we can shorten the practice'. But of course, this is not entirely the case; adjustments have to be made in methods of learning and teaching, to take account of the many ways individuals think.

D Yet in order to learn by themselves, the gifted do need some support from their teachers. Conversely, teachers who have a tendency to 'overdirect' can diminish their gifted pupils' learning autonomy. Although 'spoon-feeding' can produce extremely high examination results, these are not always followed by equally impressive life successes. Too much dependence on the teacher risks loss of autonomy and motivation to discover. However, when teachers help pupils to reflect on their own learning and thinking activities, they increase their pupils' self-regulation. For a young child, it may be just the simple question 'What have you learned today?' which helps them to recognise what they are doing. Given that a fundamental goal of education is to transfer the control of learning from teachers to pupils, improving pupils' learning to learn techniques should be a major outcome of the school experience, especially for the highly competent. There are quite a number of new methods which can help, such as child-initiated learning, ability-peer tutoring, etc. Such practices have been found to be particularly useful for bright children from deprived areas.

E But scientific progress is not all theoretical, knowledge is also vital to outstanding performance: individuals who know a great deal about a specific domain will achieve at a higher level than those who do not (Elshout, 1995). Research with creative scientists by Simonton (1988) brought him to the conclusion that above a certain high level, characteristics such as independence seemed to contribute *more* to reaching the highest levels of expertise than intellectual skills, due to the great demands of effort and time needed for learning and practice. Creativity in all forms can be seen as expertise mixed with a high level of motivation (Weisberg, 1993).

F To sum up, learning is affected by emotions of both the individual and significant others. Positive emotions facilitate the creative aspects of learning and negative emotions inhibit it. Fear, for example, can limit the development of curiosity, which is a strong force in scientific advance, because it motivates problem-solving behaviour. In Boekaerts' (1991) review of emotion in the learning of very high IQ and highly achieving children, she found emotional forces in harness. They were not only curious, but often had a strong desire to control their environment, improve their learning efficiency, and increase their own learning resources.

Questions 14–17

Reading Passage 2 has six paragraphs, **A–F**.

Which paragraph contains the following information?

*Write the correct letter, **A–F**, in boxes 14–17 on your answer sheet.*

NB *You may use any letter more than once.*

14 a reference to the influence of the domestic background on the gifted child

15 reference to what can be lost if learners are given too much guidance

16 a reference to the damaging effects of anxiety

17 examples of classroom techniques which favour socially-disadvantaged children

Questions 18–22

Look at the following statements (Questions 18–22) and the list of people below.

*Match each statement with the correct person or people, **A–E**.*

*Write the correct letter, **A–E**, in boxes 18–22 on your answer sheet.*

18 Less time can be spent on exercises with gifted pupils who produce accurate work.

19 Self-reliance is a valuable tool that helps gifted students reach their goals.

20 Gifted children know how to channel their feelings to assist their learning.

21 The very gifted child benefits from appropriate support from close relatives.

22 Really successful students have learnt a considerable amount about their subject.

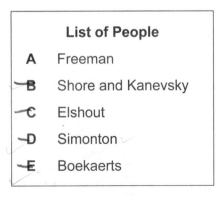

List of People
A   Freeman
B   Shore and Kanevsky
C   Elshout
D   Simonton
E   Boekaerts

Questions 23–26

Complete the sentences below.

*Choose **NO MORE THAN TWO WORDS** from the passage for each answer.*

Write your answers in boxes 23–26 on your answer sheet.

23 One study found a strong connection between children's IQ and the availability of .... and .... at home.

24 Children of average ability seem to need more direction from teachers because they do not have ....

25 Metacognition involves children understanding their own learning strategies, as well as developing ....

26 Teachers who rely on what is known as .... often produce sets of impressive grades in class tests.

READING PASSAGE 3

*You should spend about 20 minutes on **Questions 27–40**, which are based on Reading Passage 3 below.*

Museums of fine art and their public

The fact that people go to the Louvre museum in Paris to see the original painting *Mona Lisa* when they can see a reproduction anywhere leads us to question some assumptions about the role of museums of fine art in today's world

One of the most famous works of art in the world is Leonardo da Vinci's *Mona Lisa*. Nearly everyone who goes to see the original will already be familiar with it from reproductions, but they accept that fine art is more rewardingly viewed in its original form.

However, if *Mona Lisa* was a famous novel, few people would bother to go to a museum to read the writer's actual manuscript rather than a printed reproduction. This might be explained by the fact that the novel has evolved precisely because of technological developments that made it possible to print out huge numbers of texts, whereas oil paintings have always been produced as unique objects. In addition, it could be argued that the practice of interpreting or 'reading' each medium follows different conventions. With novels, the reader attends mainly to the meaning of words rather than the way they are printed on the page, whereas the 'reader' of a painting must attend just as closely to the material form of marks and shapes in the picture as to any ideas they may signify.

Yet it has always been possible to make very accurate facsimiles of pretty well any fine art work. The seven surviving versions of *Mona Lisa* bear witness to the fact that in the 16th century, artists seemed perfectly content to assign the reproduction of their creations to their workshop apprentices as regular 'bread and butter' work. And today the task of reproducing pictures is incomparably more simple and reliable, with reprographic techniques that allow the production of high-quality prints made exactly to the original scale, with faithful colour values, and even with duplication of the surface relief of the painting.

But despite an implicit recognition that the spread of good reproductions can be culturally valuable, museums continue to promote the special status of original work.

Unfortunately, this seems to place severe limitations on the kind of experience offered to visitors.

One limitation is related to the way the museum presents its exhibits. As repositories of unique historical objects, art museums are often called 'treasure houses'. We are reminded of this even before we view a collection by the presence of security guards, attendants, ropes and display cases to keep us away from the exhibits. In many cases, the architectural style of the building further reinforces that notion. In addition, a major collection like that of London's

National Gallery is housed in numerous rooms, each with dozens of works, any one of which is likely to be worth more than all the average visitor possesses. In a society that judges the personal status of the individual so much by their material worth, it is therefore difficult not to be impressed by one's own relative 'worthlessness' in such an environment.

Furthermore, consideration of the 'value' of the original work in its treasure house setting impresses upon the viewer that, since these works were originally produced, they have been assigned a huge monetary value by some person or institution more powerful than themselves. Evidently, nothing the viewer thinks about the work is going to alter that value, and so today's viewer is deterred from trying to extend that spontaneous, immediate, self-reliant kind of reading which would originally have met the work.

The visitor may then be struck by the strangeness of seeing such diverse paintings, drawings and sculptures brought together in an environment for which they were not originally created. This 'displacement effect' is further heightened by the sheer volume of exhibits. In the case of a major collection, there are probably more works on display than we could realistically view in weeks or even months.

This is particularly distressing because time seems to be a vital factor in the appreciation of all art forms. A fundamental difference between paintings and other art forms is that there is no prescribed time over which a painting is viewed. By contrast, the audience encounters an opera or a play over a specific time, which is the duration of the performance. Similarly, novels and poems are read in a prescribed temporal sequence, whereas a picture has no clear place at which to start viewing, or at which to finish. Thus art works themselves encourage us to view them superficially, without appreciating the richness of detail and labour that is involved.

Consequently, the dominant critical approach becomes that of the art historian, a specialised academic approach devoted to 'discovering the meaning' of art within the cultural context of its time. This is in perfect harmony with the museum's function, since the approach is dedicated to seeking out and conserving 'authentic', 'original' readings of the exhibits. Again, this seems to put paid to that spontaneous, participatory criticism which can be found in abundance in criticism of classic works of literature, but is absent from most art history.

The displays of art museums serve as a warning of what critical practices can emerge when spontaneous criticism is suppressed. The museum public, like any other audience, experience art more rewardingly when given the confidence to express their views. If appropriate works of fine art could be rendered permanently accessible to the public by means of high-fidelity reproductions, as literature and music already are, the public may feel somewhat less in awe of them. Unfortunately, that may be too much to ask from those who seek to maintain and control the art establishment.

Questions 27–31

*Complete the summary using the list of words, **A–L**, below.*

*Write the correct letter, **A–L**, in boxes 27–31 on your answer sheet.*

The value attached to original works of art

People go to art museums because they accept the value of seeing an original work of art. But they do not go to museums to read original manuscripts of novels, perhaps because the availability of novels has depended on **27** .... for so long, and also because with novels, the **28** .... are the most important thing.

However, in historical times artists such as Leonardo were happy to instruct **29** .... to produce copies of their work and these days new methods of reproduction allow excellent replication of surface relief features as well as colour and **30** ....

It is regrettable that museums still promote the superiority of original works of art, since this may not be in the interests of the **31** ....

A	institution	B	mass production	C	mechanical processes
D	public	E	paints	F	artist
G	size	H	underlying ideas	I	basic technology
J	readers	K	picture frames	L	assistants

Questions 32–35

*Choose the correct letter, **A**, **B**, **C** or **D**.*

Write the correct letter in boxes 32–35 on your answer sheet.

32 The writer mentions London's National Gallery to illustrate

    A   the undesirable cost to a nation of maintaining a huge collection of art.
    B   the conflict that may arise in society between financial and artistic values.
    C   the negative effect a museum can have on visitors' opinions of themselves.
    D   the need to put individual well-being above large-scale artistic schemes.

33 The writer says that today, viewers may be unwilling to criticise a work because

    A   they lack the knowledge needed to support an opinion.
    B   they fear it may have financial implications.
    C   they have no real concept of the work's value.
    D   they feel their personal reaction is of no significance.

34 According to the writer, the 'displacement effect' on the visitor is caused by

    A   the variety of works on display and the way they are arranged.
    B   the impossibility of viewing particular works of art over a long period.
    C   the similar nature of the paintings and the lack of great works.
    D   the inappropriate nature of the individual works selected for exhibition.

35 The writer says that unlike other forms of art, a painting does not

    A   involve direct contact with an audience.
    B   require a specific location for a performance.
    C   need the involvement of other professionals.
    D   have a specific beginning or end.

Questions 36–40

Do the following statements agree with the views of the writer in Reading Passage 3?

In boxes 36–40 on your answer sheet, write

> **YES**   *if the statement agrees with the views of the writer*
> **NO**   *if the statement contradicts the views of the writer*
> **NOT GIVEN**   *if it is impossible to say what the writer thinks about this*

36   Art history should focus on discovering the meaning of art using a range of media.

37   The approach of art historians conflicts with that of art museums.

38   People should be encouraged to give their opinions openly on works of art.

39   Reproductions of <u>fine</u> art should only be sold to the public if they are of high quality.

40   In the future, those with power are likely to encourage more people to enjoy art.

WRITING

WRITING TASK 1

You should spend about 20 minutes on this task.

The tables below give information about sales of Fairtrade*-labelled coffee and bananas in 1999 and 2004 in five European countries.

Summarise the information by selecting and reporting the main features, and make comparisons where relevant.

Write at least 150 words.

Sales of Fairtrade-labelled coffee and bananas (1999 & 2004)

Coffee	1999 (millions of euros)	2004 (millions of euros)
UK	1.5	20
Switzerland	3	6
Denmark	1.8	2
Belgium	1	1.7
Sweden	0.8	1

Bananas	1999 (millions of euros)	2004 (millions of euros)
Switzerland	15	47
UK	1	5.5
Belgium	0.6	4
Sweden	1.8	1
Denmark	2	0.9

* Fairtrade: a category of products for which farmers from developing countries have been paid an officially agreed fair price.

WRITING TASK 2

You should spend about 40 minutes on this task.

Write about the following topic:

Some people think that all university students should study whatever they like. Others believe that they should only be allowed to study subjects that will be useful in the future, such as those related to science and technology.

Discuss both these views and give your own opinion.

Give reasons for your answer and include any relevant examples from your own knowledge or experience.

Write at least 250 words.

SPEAKING

PART 1

The examiner asks the candidate about him/herself, his/her home, work or studies and other familiar topics.

EXAMPLE

Music

- What types of music do you like to listen to? [Why?]
- At what times of day do you like to listen to music? [Why?]
- Did you learn to play a musical instrument when you were a child? [Why/Why not?]
- Do you think all children should learn to play a musical instrument? [Why/Why not?]

PART 2

Describe a shop near where you live that you sometimes use.

You should say:
> **what sorts of product or service it sells**
> **what the shop looks like**
> **where it is located**
and explain why you use this shop.

You will have to talk about the topic for one to two minutes.
You have one minute to think about what you are going to say.
You can make some notes to help you if you wish.

PART 3

Discussion topics:

Local business

Example questions:
What types of local business are there in your neighbourhood? Are there any restaurants, shops or dentists for example?
Do you think local businesses are important for a neighbourhood? In what way?
How do large shopping malls and commercial centres affect small local businesses? Why do you think that is?

People and business

Example questions:
Why do some people want to start their own business?
Are there any disadvantages to running a business? Which is the most serious?
What are the most important qualities that a good business person needs? Why is that?

Test 3

SECTION 1   *Questions 1–10*

Complete the form below.

*Write **ONE WORD AND/OR A NUMBER** for each answer.*

**Early Learning Childcare Centre
Enrolment Form**

Example

Parent or guardian: Carol ....Smith...........

Personal Details

Child's name: Kate

Age: **1** ....

Address: **2** .... Road, Woodside, 4032

Phone: 3345 9865

Childcare Information

Days enrolled for: Monday and **3** ....

Start time: **4** .... am

Childcare group: the **5** .... group

Which meal/s are required each day? **6** ....

Medical conditions: needs **7** ....

Emergency contact: Jenny **8** .... Phone: 3346 7523

Relationship to child: **9** ....

Fees

Will pay each **10** ....

SECTION 2   *Questions 11–20*

Questions 11 and 12

*Choose **TWO** letters, **A–E**.*

Which **TWO** things does Alice say about the Dolphin Conservation Trust?

- **A**   Children make up most of the membership.
- **B**   It's the country's largest conservation organisation.
- **C**   It helps finance campaigns for changes in fishing practices.
- **D**   It employs several dolphin experts full-time.
- **E**   Volunteers help in various ways.

Questions 13–15

*Choose the correct letter, **A**, **B**, or **C**.*

13   Why is Alice so pleased the Trust has won the Charity Commission award?

- **A**   It has brought in extra money.
- **B**   It made the work of the trust better known.
- **C**   It has attracted more members.

14   Alice says oil exploration causes problems to dolphins because of

- **A**   noise.
- **B**   oil leaks.
- **C**   movement of ships.

15   Alice became interested in dolphins when

- **A**   she saw one swimming near her home.
- **B**   she heard a speaker at her school.
- **C**   she read a book about them.

Questions 16–20

Which dolphin does Alice make each of the following comments about?

*Write the correct letter, **A**, **B**, **C** or **D**, next to questions 16–20.*

	Dolphins
A	Moondancer
B	Echo
C	Kiwi
D	Samson

Comments

16   It has not been seen this year.   ....

17   It is photographed more than the others.   ....

18   It is always very energetic.   ....

19   It is the newest one in the scheme.   ....

20   It has an unusual shape.   ....

SECTION 3   *Questions 21–30*

Questions 21–25

Choose the correct letter, A, B or C.

Theatre Studies Course

21   What helped Rob to prepare to play the character of a doctor?

    A   the stories his grandfather told him
    B   the times when he watched his grandfather working
    C   the way he imagined his grandfather at work

22   In the play's first scene, the boredom of village life was suggested by

    A   repetition of words and phrases.
    B   scenery painted in dull colours.
    C   long pauses within conversations.

23   What has Rob learned about himself through working in a group?

    A   He likes to have clear guidelines.
    B   He copes well with stress.
    C   He thinks he is a good leader.

24   To support the production, research material was used which described

    A   political developments.
    B   changing social attitudes.
    C   economic transformations.

25   What problem did the students overcome in the final rehearsal?

    A   one person forgetting their words
    B   an equipment failure
    C   the injury of one character

Questions 26–30

What action is needed for the following stages in doing the 'year abroad' option?

*Choose **FIVE** answers from the box and write the correct letter, **A–G**, next to questions 26–30.*

Action
A   be on time
B   get a letter of recommendation
C   plan for the final year
D   make sure the institution's focus is relevant
E   show ability in Theatre Studies
F   make travel arrangements and bookings
G   ask for help

Stages in doing the 'year abroad' option

26   in the second year of the course   ....

27   when first choosing where to go   ....

28   when sending in your choices   ....

29   when writing your personal statement   ....

30   when doing the year abroad   ....

SECTION 4   *Questions 31–40*

Complete the notes below.

Write ONE WORD ONLY for each answer.

'Self-regulatory focus theory' and leadership

Self-regulatory focus theory

People's focus is to approach pleasure or avoid pain
Promotion goals focus on **31** ....
Prevention goals emphasise avoiding punishment

Factors that affect people's focus

The Chronic Factor

• comes from one's **32** ....

The **33** .... Factor

• we are more likely to focus on promotion goals when with a **34** ....

• we are more likely to focus on prevention goals with our boss

How people's focus affects them

Promotion Focus: People think about an ideal version of themselves, their
35 .... and their gains.

Prevention Focus: People think about their 'ought' self and their obligations

---

Leaders

Leadership behaviour and **36** .... affects people's focus

Transformational Leaders:

- pay special attention to the **37** .... of their followers
- passionately communicate a clear **38** ....
- inspire promotion focus in followers

Transactional Leaders:

- create **39** .... to make expectations clear
- emphasise the results of a mistake
- inspire prevention focus in followers

Conclusion

Promotion Focus is good for jobs requiring **40** ....
Prevention Focus is good for work such as a surgeon
Leaders' actions affect which focus people use

READING

READING PASSAGE 1

*You should spend about 20 minutes on **Questions 1–13**, which are based on Reading Passage 1 on the following pages.*

Questions 1–4

Reading Passage 1 has five paragraphs, **A–E**.

*Choose the correct heading for paragraphs **B–E** from the list of headings below.*

*Write the correct number, **i–vii**, in boxes 1–4 on your answer sheet.*

List of Headings
i Economic and social significance of tourism
ii The development of mass tourism
iii Travel for the wealthy
iv Earning foreign exchange through tourism
v Difficulty in recognising the economic effects of tourism
vi The contribution of air travel to tourism
vii The world impact of tourism
viii The history of travel

Example	Answer
Paragraph **A**	**viii**

1   Paragraph **B**

2   Paragraph **C**

3   Paragraph **D**

4   Paragraph **E**

The Context, Meaning and Scope of Tourism

A   Travel has existed since the beginning of time, when primitive man set out, often traversing great distances in search of game, which provided the food and clothing necessary for his survival. Throughout the course of history, people have travelled for purposes of trade, religious conviction, economic gain, war, migration and other equally compelling motivations. In the Roman era, wealthy aristocrats and high government officials also travelled for pleasure. Seaside resorts located at Pompeii and Herculaneum afforded citizens the opportunity to escape to their vacation villas in order to avoid the summer heat of Rome. Travel, except during the Dark Ages, has continued to grow and, throughout recorded history, has played a vital role in the development of civilisations and their economies.

B   Tourism in the mass form as we know it today is a distinctly twentieth-century phenomenon. Historians suggest that the advent of mass tourism began in England during the industrial revolution with the rise of the middle class and the availability of relatively inexpensive transportation. The creation of the commercial airline industry following the Second World War and the subsequent development of the jet aircraft in the 1950s signalled the rapid growth and expansion of international travel. This growth led to the development of a major new industry: tourism. In turn, international tourism became the concern of a number of world governments since it not only provided new employment opportunities but also produced a means of earning foreign exchange.

C   Tourism today has grown significantly in both economic and social importance. In most industrialised countries over the past few years the fastest growth has been seen in the area of services. One of the largest segments of the service industry, although largely unrecognised as an entity in some of these countries, is travel and tourism. According to the World Travel and Tourism Council (1992), 'Travel and tourism is the largest industry in the world on virtually any economic measure including value-added capital investment, employment and tax contributions'. In 1992, the industry's gross output was estimated to be $3.5 trillion, over 12 per cent of all consumer spending. The travel and tourism industry is the world's largest employer with almost 130 million jobs, or almost 7 per cent of all employees. This industry is the world's leading industrial contributor, producing over 6 per cent of the world's gross national product and accounting for capital investment in excess of $422 billion in direct, indirect and personal taxes each year. Thus, tourism has a profound impact both on the world economy and, because of the educative effect of travel and the effects on employment, on society itself.

D   However, the major problems of the travel and tourism industry that have hidden, or obscured, its economic impact are the diversity and fragmentation of the industry itself. The travel industry includes: hotels, motels and other types of accommodation; restaurants and other food services; transportation services and facilities; amusements, attractions and other leisure facilities; gift shops and a large number of other enterprises. Since many of these businesses also serve local residents, the impact of spending by visitors can easily be overlooked or underestimated. In addition, Meis (1992) points out that the tourism industry involves concepts that have remained amorphous to both analysts and decision makers. Moreover, in all nations this problem has made it difficult for the industry to develop any type of reliable or credible tourism information base in order to estimate the contribution it makes to regional, national and global economies. However, the nature of this very diversity makes travel and tourism ideal vehicles for economic development in a wide variety of countries, regions or communities.

E   Once the exclusive province of the wealthy, travel and tourism have become an institutionalised way of life for most of the population. In fact, McIntosh and Goeldner (1990) suggest that tourism has become the largest commodity in international trade for many nations and, for a significant number of other countries, it ranks second or third. For example, tourism is the major source of income in Bermuda, Greece, Italy, Spain, Switzerland and most Caribbean countries. In addition, Hawkins and Ritchie, quoting from data published by the American Express Company, suggest that the travel and tourism industry is the number one ranked employer in the Bahamas, Brazil, Canada, France, (the former) West Germany, Hong Kong, Italy, Jamaica, Japan, Singapore, the United Kingdom and the United States. However, because of problems of definition, which directly affect statistical measurement, it is not possible with any degree of certainty to provide precise, valid or reliable data about the extent of world-wide tourism participation or its economic impact. In many cases, similar difficulties arise when attempts are made to measure domestic tourism.

Questions 5–10

Do the following statements agree with the information given in Reading Passage 1?

In boxes 5–10 on your answer sheet, write

> **TRUE**   *if the statement agrees with the information*
> **FALSE**   *if the statement contradicts the information*
> **NOT GIVEN** *if there is no information on this*

5   The largest employment figures in the world are found in the travel and tourism industry.

6   Tourism contributes over six per cent of the Australian gross national product.

7   Tourism has a social impact because it promotes recreation.

8   Two main features of the travel and tourism industry make its economic significance difficult to ascertain.

9   Visitor spending is always greater than the spending of residents in tourist areas.

10   It is easy to show statistically how tourism affects individual economies.

Questions 11–13

Complete the sentences below.

*Choose **NO MORE THAN THREE WORDS** from the passage for each answer.*

Write your answers in boxes 11–13 on your answer sheet.

11   In Greece, tourism is the most important ....

12   The travel and tourism industry in Jamaica is the major ....

13   The problems associated with measuring international tourism are often reflected in the measurement of ....

READING PASSAGE 2

*You should spend about 20 minutes on **Questions 14–26**, which are based on Reading Passage 2 below.*

Autumn leaves

Canadian writer Jay Ingram investigates the mystery of why leaves turn red in the fall

A One of the most captivating natural events of the year in many areas throughout North America is the turning of the leaves in the fall. The colours are magnificent, but the question of exactly why some trees turn yellow or orange, and others red or purple, is something which has long puzzled scientists.

B Summer leaves are green because they are full of chlorophyll, the molecule that captures sunlight and converts that energy into new building materials for the tree. As fall approaches in the northern hemisphere, the amount of solar energy available declines considerably. For many trees – evergreen conifers being an exception – the best strategy is to abandon photosynthesis* until the spring. So rather than maintaining the now redundant leaves throughout the winter, the tree saves its precious resources and discards them. But before letting its leaves go, the tree dismantles their chlorophyll molecules and ships their valuable nitrogen back into the twigs. As chlorophyll is depleted, other colours that have been dominated by it throughout the summer begin to be revealed. This unmasking explains the autumn colours of yellow and orange, but not the brilliant reds and purples of trees such as the maple or sumac.

C The source of the red is widely known: it is created by anthocyanins, water-soluble plant pigments reflecting the red to blue range of the visible spectrum. They belong to a class of sugar-based chemical compounds also known as flavonoids. What's puzzling is that anthocyanins are actually newly minted, made in the leaves at the same time as the tree is preparing to drop them. But it is hard to make sense of the manufacture of anthocyanins – why should a tree bother making new chemicals in its leaves when it's already scrambling to withdraw and preserve the ones already there?

D Some theories about anthocyanins have argued that they might act as a chemical defence against attacks by insects or fungi, or that they might attract fruit-eating birds or increase a leaf's tolerance to freezing. However there are problems with each of these theories, including the fact that leaves are red for such a relatively short period that the expense of energy needed to manufacture the anthocyanins would outweigh any anti-fungal or anti-herbivore activity achieved.

* photosynthesis: the production of new material from sunlight, water and carbon dioxide

E   It has also been proposed that trees may produce vivid red colours to convince herbivorous insects that they are healthy and robust and would be easily able to mount chemical defences against infestation. If insects paid attention to such advertisements, they might be prompted to lay their eggs on a duller, and presumably less resistant host. The flaw in this theory lies in the lack of proof to support it. No one has as yet ascertained whether more robust trees sport the brightest leaves, or whether insects make choices according to colour intensity.

F   Perhaps the most plausible suggestion as to why leaves would go to the trouble of making anthocyanins when they're busy packing up for the winter is the theory known as the 'light screen' hypothesis. It sounds paradoxical, because the idea behind this hypothesis is that the red pigment is made in autumn leaves to protect chlorophyll, the light-absorbing chemical, from *too much light*. Why does chlorophyll need protection when it is the natural world's supreme light absorber? Why protect chlorophyll at a time when the tree is breaking it down to salvage as much of it as possible?

G   Chlorophyll, although exquisitely evolved to capture the energy of sunlight, can sometimes be overwhelmed by it, especially in situations of drought, low temperatures, or nutrient deficiency. Moreover, the problem of oversensitivity to light is even more acute in the fall, when the leaf is busy preparing for winter by dismantling its internal machinery. The energy absorbed by the chlorophyll molecules of the unstable autumn leaf is not immediately channelled into useful products and processes, as it would be in an intact summer leaf. The weakened fall leaf then becomes vulnerable to the highly destructive effects of the oxygen created by the excited chlorophyll molecules.

H   Even if you had never suspected that this is what was going on when leaves turn red, there are clues out there. One is straightforward: on many trees, the leaves that are the reddest are those on the side of the tree which gets most sun. Not only that, but the red is brighter on the upper side of the leaf. It has also been recognised for decades that the best conditions for intense red colours are dry, sunny days and cool nights, conditions that nicely match those that make leaves susceptible to excess light. And finally, trees such as maples usually get much redder the more north you travel in the northern hemisphere. It's colder there, they're more stressed, their chlorophyll is more sensitive and it needs more sunblock.

I   What is still not fully understood, however, is why some trees resort to producing red pigments while others don't bother, and simply reveal their orange or yellow hues. Do these trees have other means at their disposal to prevent overexposure to light in autumn? Their story, though not as spectacular to the eye, will surely turn out to be as subtle and as complex.

Questions 14–18

Reading Passage 2 has nine paragraphs, **A–I**.

Which paragraph contains the following information?

*Write the correct letter, **A–I**, in boxes 14–18 on your answer sheet.*

NB *You may use any letter more than once.*

14   a description of the substance responsible for the red colouration of leaves

15   the reason why trees drop their leaves in autumn

16   some evidence to confirm a theory about the purpose of the red leaves

17   an explanation of the function of chlorophyll

18   a suggestion that the red colouration in leaves could serve as a warning signal

Questions 19–22

Complete the notes below.

*Choose **ONE WORD ONLY** from the passage for each answer.*

Write your answers in boxes 19–22 on your answer sheet.

Why believe the 'light screen' hypothesis?

- The most vividly coloured red leaves are found on the side of the tree facing the **19** ....

- The **20** .... surfaces of leaves contain the most red pigment.

- Red leaves are most abundant when daytime weather conditions are **21** .... and sunny.

- The intensity of the red colour of leaves increases as you go further **22** ....

Questions 23–25

Do the following statements agree with the information given in Reading Passage 2?

In boxes 23–25 on your answer sheet, write

> **TRUE**   *if the statement agrees with the information*
> **FALSE**   *if the statement contradicts the information*
> **NOT GIVEN**   *if there is no information on this*

23   It is likely that the red pigments help to protect the leaf from freezing temperatures.

24   The 'light screen' hypothesis would initially seem to contradict what is known about chlorophyll.

25   Leaves which turn colours other than red are more likely to be damaged by sunlight.

Question 26

*Choose the correct letter **A**, **B**, **C** or **D**.*

Write the correct letter in box 26 on your answer sheet.

For which of the following questions does the writer offer an explanation?

   A   why conifers remain green in winter
   B   how leaves turn orange and yellow in autumn
   C   how herbivorous insects choose which trees to lay their eggs in
   D   why anthocyanins are restricted to certain trees

READING PASSAGE 3

*You should spend about 20 minutes on **Questions 27–40**, which are based on Reading Passage 3 below.*

Beyond the blue horizon

Ancient voyagers who settled the far-flung islands of the Pacific Ocean

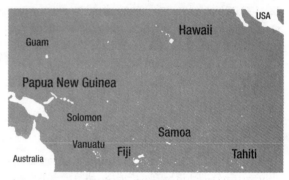

An important archaeological discovery on the island of Éfaté in the Pacific archipelago of Vanuatu has revealed traces of an ancient seafaring people, the distant ancestors of today's Polynesians. The site came to light only by chance. An agricultural worker, digging in the grounds of a derelict plantation, scraped open a grave – the first of dozens in a burial ground some 3,000 years old. It is the oldest cemetery ever found in the Pacific islands, and it harbors the remains of an ancient people archaeologists call the Lapita.

They were daring blue-water adventurers who used basic canoes to rove across the ocean. But they were not just explorers. They were also pioneers who carried with them everything they would need to build new lives – their livestock, taro seedlings and stone tools. Within the span of several centuries, the Lapita stretched the boundaries of their world from the jungle-clad volcanoes of Papua New Guinea to the loneliest coral outliers of Tonga.

The Lapita left precious few clues about themselves, but Éfaté expands the volume of data available to researchers dramatically. The remains of 62 individuals have been uncovered so far, and archaeologists were also thrilled to find six complete Lapita pots. Other items included a Lapita burial urn with modeled birds arranged on the rim as though peering down at the human remains sealed inside. 'It's an important discovery,' says Matthew Spriggs, professor of archaeology at the Australian National University and head of the international team digging up the site, 'for it conclusively identifies the remains as Lapita.'

DNA teased from these human remains may help answer one of the most puzzling questions in Pacific anthropology: did all Pacific islanders spring from one source or many? Was there only one outward migration from a single point in Asia, or several from different points? 'This represents the best opportunity we've had yet,' says Spriggs, 'to find out who the Lapita actually were, where they came from, and who their closest descendants are today.'

There is one stubborn question for which archaeology has yet to provide any answers: how did the Lapita accomplish the ancient equivalent of a moon landing, many times over? No-one has found one of their canoes or any rigging, which could reveal how the canoes were sailed. Nor do the oral histories and traditions of later Polynesians offer any insights, for they turn into myths long before they reach as far back in time as the Lapita.

'All we can say for certain is that the Lapita had canoes that were capable of ocean voyages, and they had the ability to sail them,' says Geoff Irwin, a professor of archaeology at the University of Auckland. Those sailing skills, he says, were developed and passed down over thousands of years by earlier mariners who worked their way through the archipelagoes of the western Pacific, making short crossings to nearby islands. The real adventure didn't begin, however, until their Lapita descendants sailed out of sight of land, with empty horizons on every side. This must have been as difficult for them as landing on the moon is for us today. Certainly it distinguished them from their ancestors, but what gave them the courage to launch out on such risky voyages?

The Lapita's thrust into the Pacific was eastward, against the prevailing trade winds, Irwin notes. Those nagging headwinds, he argues, may have been the key to their success. 'They could sail out for days into the unknown and assess the area, secure in the knowledge that if they didn't find anything, they could turn about and catch a swift ride back on the trade winds. This is what would have made the whole thing work.' Once out there, skilled seafarers would have detected abundant leads to follow to land: seabirds, coconuts and twigs carried out to sea by the tides, and the afternoon pile-up of clouds on the horizon which often indicates an island in the distance.

For returning explorers, successful or not, the geography of their own archipelagoes would have provided a safety net. Without this to go by, overshooting their home ports, getting lost and sailing off into eternity would have been all too easy. Vanuatu, for example, stretches more than 500 miles in a northwest-southeast trend, its scores of intervisible islands forming a backstop for mariners riding the trade winds home.

All this presupposes one essential detail, says Atholl Anderson, professor of prehistory at the Australian National University: the Lapita had mastered the advanced art of sailing against the wind. 'And there's no proof they could do any such thing,' Anderson says. 'There has been this assumption they did, and people have built canoes to re-create those early voyages based on that assumption. But nobody has any idea what their canoes looked like or how they were rigged.'

Rather than give all the credit to human skill, Anderson invokes the winds of chance. El Niño, the same climate disruption that affects the Pacific today, may have helped scatter the Lapita, Anderson suggests. He points out that climate data obtained from slow-growing corals around the Pacific indicate a series of unusually frequent El Niños around the time of the Lapita expansion. By reversing the regular east-to-west flow of the trade winds for weeks at a time, these 'super El Niños' might have taken the Lapita on long unplanned voyages.

However they did it, the Lapita spread themselves a third of the way across the Pacific, then called it quits for reasons known only to them. Ahead lay the vast emptiness of the central Pacific and perhaps they were too thinly stretched to venture farther. They probably never numbered more than a few thousand in total, and in their rapid migration eastward they encountered hundreds of islands – more than 300 in Fiji alone.

Questions 27–31

*Complete the summary using the list of words and phrases, **A–J**, below.*

*Write the correct letter, **A–J**, in boxes 27–31 on your answer sheet.*

The Éfaté burial site

A 3,000-year-old burial ground of a seafaring people called the Lapita has been found on an abandoned **27** .... on the Pacific island of Éfaté. The cemetery, which is a significant **28** .... , was uncovered accidentally by an agricultural worker.

The Lapita explored and colonised many Pacific islands over several centuries. They took many things with them on their voyages including **29** .... and tools.

The burial ground increases the amount of information about the Lapita available to scientists. A team of researchers, led by Matthew Spriggs from the Australian National University, are helping with the excavation of the site. Spriggs believes the **30** .... which was found at the site is very important since it confirms that the **31** .... found inside are Lapita.

A	proof
B	plantation
C	harbour
D	bones
E	data
F	archaeological discovery
G	burial urn
H	source
I	animals
J	maps

Questions 32–35

*Choose the correct letter, **A**, **B**, **C** or **D**.*

Write the correct letter in boxes 32–35 on your answer sheet.

32 According to the writer, there are difficulties explaining how the Lapita accomplished their journeys because

    A   the canoes that have been discovered offer relatively few clues.
    B   archaeologists have shown limited interest in this area of research.
    C   little information relating to this period can be relied upon for accuracy.
    D   technological advances have altered the way such achievements are viewed.

33 According to the sixth paragraph, what was extraordinary about the Lapita?

    A   They sailed beyond the point where land was visible.
    B   Their cultural heritage discouraged the expression of fear.
    C   They were able to build canoes that withstood ocean voyages.
    D   Their navigational skills were passed on from one generation to the next.

34 What does 'This' refer to in the seventh paragraph?

    A   the Lapita's seafaring talent
    B   the Lapita's ability to detect signs of land
    C   the Lapita's extensive knowledge of the region
    D   the Lapita's belief they would be able to return home

35 According to the eighth paragraph, how was the geography of the region significant?

    A   It played an important role in Lapita culture.
    B   It meant there were relatively few storms at sea.
    C   It provided a navigational aid for the Lapita.
    D   It made a large number of islands habitable.

Questions 36–40

Do the following statements agree with the views of the writer in Reading Passage 3?

In boxes 36–40 on your answer sheet, write

> **YES**   if the statement agrees with the views of the writer
> **NO**   if the statement contradicts the views of the writer
> **NOT GIVEN** if it is impossible to say what the writer thinks about this

36   It is now clear that the Lapita could sail into a prevailing wind.

37   Extreme climate conditions may have played a role in Lapita migration.

38   The Lapita learnt to predict the duration of El Niños.

39   It remains unclear why the Lapita halted their expansion across the Pacific.

40   It is likely that the majority of Lapita settled on Fiji.

WRITING

WRITING TASK 1

You should spend about 20 minutes on this task.

The charts below show what UK graduate and postgraduate students who did not go into full-time work did after leaving college in 2008.

Summarise the information by selecting and reporting the main features, and make comparisons where relevant.

Write at least 150 words.

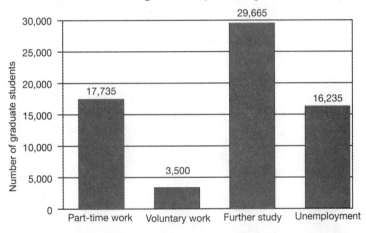

Destination of UK graduates (excluding full-time work) 2008

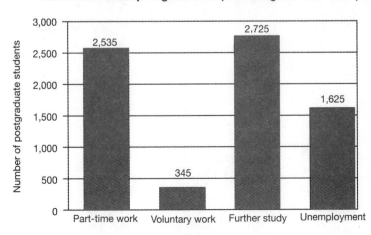

Destination of UK postgraduates (excluding full-time work) 2008

WRITING TASK 2

You should spend about 40 minutes on this task.

Write about the following topic:

Countries are becoming more and more similar because people are able to buy the same products anywhere in the world.

Do you think this is a positive or negative development?

Give reasons for your answer and include any relevant examples from your own knowledge or experience.

Write at least 250 words.

SPEAKING

PART 1

The examiner asks the candidate about him/herself, his/her home, work or studies and other familiar topics.

EXAMPLE

Travel

- Do you enjoy travelling? [Why/Why not?]
- Have you done much travelling? [Why/Why not?]
- Do you think it's better to travel alone or with other people? [Why?]
- Where would you like to travel in the future? [Why?]

PART 2

> **Describe a child that you know.**
>
> **You should say:**
> **who this child is and how often you see him or her**
> **how old this child is**
> **what he or she is like**
> **and explain what you feel about this child.**

You will have to talk about the topic for one to two minutes.
You have one minute to think about what you are going to say.
You can make some notes to help you if you wish.

PART 3

Discussion topics:

Relationships between parents and children

Example questions:
How much time do children spend with their parents in your country? Do you think that is enough?
How important do you think spending time together is for the relationships between parents and children? Why?
Have relationships between parents and children changed in recent years? Why do you think that is?

Children's free-time activities

Example questions:
What are the most popular free-time activities with children today?
Do you think the free-time activities children do today are good for their health? Why is that?
How do you think children's activities will change in the future? Will this be a positive change?

Test 4

SECTION 1   Questions 1–10

Questions 1–6

Complete the notes below.

Write **ONE WORD ONLY** for each answer.

THORNDYKE'S BUILDERS
Example   Customer heard about Thorndyke's from a ....<u>friend</u>.............

Name: Edith **1** ....
 	
 Address: Flat 4,
 	
                     2 .... Park Flats
 	
                     (Behind the **3** ....)
 	
 Phone number: 875934
 	
 Best time to contact customer: during the **4** ....
 	
 Where to park: opposite entrance next to the **5** ....
 	
 Needs full quote showing all the jobs and the **6** ....

Questions 7–10

Complete the table below.

*Write **ONE WORD ONLY** for each answer.*

Area	Work to be done	Notes
Kitchen	Replace the **7** .... in the door	Fix tomorrow
	Paint wall above the **8**	Strip paint and plaster approximately one **9** .... in advance
Garden	One **10** .... needs replacing (end of garden)	

SECTION 2   *Questions 11–20*

Questions 11–15

Choose the correct letter, A, B or C.

MANHAM PORT

11   Why did a port originally develop at Manham?

   A   It was safe from enemy attack.
   B   It was convenient for river transport.
   C   It had a good position on the sea coast.

12   What caused Manham's sudden expansion during the Industrial Revolution?

   A   the improvement in mining techniques
   B   the increase in demand for metals
   C   the discovery of tin in the area

13   Why did rocks have to be sent away from Manham to be processed?

   A   shortage of fuel
   B   poor transport systems
   C   lack of skills among local people

14   What happened when the port declined in the twentieth century?

   A   The workers went away.
   B   Traditional skills were lost.
   C   Buildings were used for new purposes.

15   What did the Manham Trust hope to do?

   A   discover the location of the original port
   B   provide jobs for the unemployed
   C   rebuild the port complex

Questions 16–20

Complete the table below.

Write **NO MORE THAN TWO WORDS** *for each answer.*

Tourist attractions in Manham		
Place	**Features and activities**	**Advice**
copper mine	specially adapted miners' **16** .... take visitors into the mountain	the mine is **17** .... and enclosed – unsuitable for children and animals
village school	classrooms and a special exhibition of **18**	a **19** .... is recommended
'The George' (old sailing ship)	the ship's wheel (was lost but has now been restored)	children shouldn't use the **20** ....

SECTION 3   *Questions 21–30*

Questions 21 and 22

*Choose **TWO** letters, **A–E**.*

Which **TWO** skills did Laura improve as a result of her work placement?

    A   communication
    B   design
    C   IT
    D   marketing
    E   organisation

Questions 23 and 24

*Choose **TWO** letters, **A–E**.*

Which **TWO** immediate benefits did the company get from Laura's work placement?

    A   updates for its software
    B   cost savings
    C   an improved image
    D   new clients
    E   a growth in sales

Questions 25–30

What source of information should Tim use at each of the following stages of the work placement?

*Choose **SIX** answers from the box and write the correct letter, **A–G**, next to questions 25–30.*

Sources of information

A company manager

B company's personnel department

C personal tutor

D psychology department

E mentor

F university careers officer

G internet

Stages of the work placement procedure

25 obtaining booklet   ....

26 discussing options   ....

27 getting updates   ....

28 responding to invitation for interview   ....

29 informing about outcome of interview   ....

30 requesting a reference   ....

SECTION 4   *Questions 31–40*

Questions 31–33

*Choose the correct letter, **A**, **B** or **C**.*

Nanotechnology: technology on a small scale

31 The speaker says that one problem with nanotechnology is that

   A   it could threaten our way of life.
   B   it could be used to spy on people.
   C   it is misunderstood by the public.

32 According to the speaker, some scientists believe that nano-particles

   A   should be restricted to secure environments.
   B   should be used with more caution.
   C   should only be developed for essential products.

33 In the speaker's opinion, research into nanotechnology

   A   has yet to win popular support.
   B   could be seen as unethical.
   C   ought to be continued.

Questions 34–40

Complete the notes below.

Write ONE WORD ONLY for each answer.

Uses of Nanotechnology

Transport

- Nanotechnology could allow the development of stronger **34** ....

- Planes would be much lighter in weight.

- **35** .... travel will be made available to the masses.

Technology

- Computers will be even smaller, faster, and will have a greater
  36 ....

- **37** .... energy will become more affordable.

The Environment

- Nano-robots could rebuild the ozone layer.

- Pollutants such as **38** .... could be removed from water
  more easily.

- There will be no **39** .... from manufacturing.

Health and Medicine

- New methods of food production could eradicate famine.

- Analysis of medical **40** .... will be speeded up.

- Life expectancy could be increased.

READING PASSAGE 1

*You should spend about 20 minutes on **Questions 1–13**, which are based on Reading Passage 1 below.*

The megafires of California

Drought, housing expansion, and oversupply of tinder make for bigger, hotter fires in the western United States

Wildfires are becoming an increasing menace in the western United States, with Southern California being the hardest hit area. There's a reason fire squads battling more frequent blazes in Southern California are having such difficulty containing the flames, despite better preparedness than ever and decades of experience fighting fires fanned by the 'Santa Ana Winds'. The wildfires themselves, experts say, are generally hotter, faster, and spread more erratically than in the past.

Megafires, also called 'siege fires', are the increasingly frequent blazes that burn 500,000 acres or more – 10 times the size of the average forest fire of 20 years ago. Some recent wildfires are among the biggest ever in California in terms of acreage burned, according to state figures and news reports.

One explanation for the trend to more superhot fires is that the region, which usually has dry summers, has had significantly below normal precipitation in many recent years. Another reason, experts say, is related to the century-long policy of the US Forest Service to stop wildfires as quickly as possible. The unintentional consequence has been to halt the natural eradication of underbrush, now the primary fuel for megafires.

Three other factors contribute to the trend, they add. First is climate change, marked by a 1-degree Fahrenheit rise in average yearly temperature across the western states. Second is fire seasons that on average are 78 days longer than they were 20 years ago. Third is increased construction of homes in wooded areas.

'We are increasingly building our homes in fire-prone ecosystems,' says Dominik Kulakowski, adjunct professor of biology at Clark University Graduate School of Geography in Worcester, Massachusetts. 'Doing that in many of the forests of the western US is like building homes on the side of an active volcano.'

In California, where population growth has averaged more than 600,000 a year for at least a decade, more residential housing is being built. 'What once was open space is now residential homes providing fuel to make fires burn with greater intensity,' says Terry McHale of the California Department of Forestry firefighters' union. 'With so much dryness, so many communities to catch fire, so many fronts to fight, it becomes an almost incredible job.'

That said, many experts give California high marks for making progress on preparedness in recent years, after some of the largest fires in state history scorched thousands of acres, burned thousands of homes, and killed numerous people. Stung in the past by criticism of bungling that allowed fires to spread when they might have been contained, personnel are meeting the peculiar challenges of neighborhood – and canyon- hopping fires better than previously, observers say.

State promises to provide more up-to-date engines, planes, and helicopters to fight fires have been fulfilled. Firefighters' unions that in the past complained of dilapidated equipment, old fire engines, and insufficient blueprints for fire safety are now praising the state's commitment, noting that funding for firefighting has increased, despite huge cuts in many other programs. 'We are pleased that the current state administration has been very proactive in its support of us, and [has] come through with budgetary support of the infrastructure needs we have long sought,' says Mr. McHale of the firefighters' union.

Besides providing money to upgrade the fire engines that must traverse the mammoth state and wind along serpentine canyon roads, the state has invested in better command-and-control facilities as well as in the strategies to run them. 'In the fire sieges of earlier years, we found that other jurisdictions and states were willing to offer mutual-aid help, but we were not able to communicate adequately with them,' says Kim Zagaris, chief of the state's Office of Emergency Services Fire and Rescue Branch. After a commission examined and revamped communications procedures, the statewide response 'has become far more professional and responsive,' he says. There is a sense among both government officials and residents that the speed, dedication, and coordination of firefighters from several states and jurisdictions are resulting in greater efficiency than in past 'siege fire' situations.

In recent years, the Southern California region has improved building codes, evacuation procedures, and procurement of new technology. 'I am extraordinarily impressed by the improvements we have witnessed,' says Randy Jacobs, a Southern California-based lawyer who has had to evacuate both his home and business to escape wildfires. 'Notwithstanding all the damage that will continue to be caused by wildfires, we will no longer suffer the loss of life endured in the past because of the fire prevention and firefighting measures that have been put in place,' he says.

Questions 1–6

Complete the notes below.

*Choose **ONE WORD AND/OR A NUMBER** from the passage for each answer.*

Write your answers in boxes 1–6 on your answer sheet.

Wildfires

- Characteristics of wildfires and wildfire conditions today compared to the past:

    - occurrence: more frequent

    - temperature: hotter

    - speed: faster

    - movement: **1** .... more unpredictably

    - size of fires: **2** .... greater on average than two decades ago

- Reasons wildfires cause more damage today compared to the past:

    - rainfall: **3** .... average

    - more brush to act as **4** ....

    - increase in yearly temperature

    - extended fire **5** ....

    - more building of **6** .... in vulnerable places

---

Questions 7–13

Do the following statements agree with the information given in Reading Passage 1?

In boxes 7–13 on your answer sheet, write

> **TRUE**   *if the statement agrees with the information*
> **FALSE**   *if the statement contradicts the information*
> **NOT GIVEN** *if there is no information on this*

7   The amount of open space in California has diminished over the last ten years.

8   Many experts believe California has made little progress in readying itself to fight fires.

9   Personnel in the past have been criticised for mishandling fire containment.

10 California has replaced a range of firefighting tools.

11 More firefighters have been hired to improve fire-fighting capacity.

12 Citizens and government groups disapprove of the efforts of different states and agencies working together.

13 Randy Jacobs believes that loss of life from fires will continue at the same levels, despite changes made.

READING PASSAGE 2

*You should spend about 20 minutes on **Questions 14–26**, which are based on Reading Passage 2 below.*

Second nature

Your personality isn't necessarily set in stone. With a little experimentation, people can reshape their temperaments and inject passion, optimism, joy and courage into their lives

A   Psychologists have long held that a person's character cannot undergo a transformation in any meaningful way and that the key traits of personality are determined at a very young age. However, researchers have begun looking more closely at ways we *can* change. Positive psychologists have identified 24 qualities we admire, such as loyalty and kindness, and are studying them to find out why they come so naturally to some people. What they're discovering is that many of these qualities amount to habitual behaviour that determines the way we respond to the world. The good news is that all this can be learned.

Some qualities are less challenging to develop than others, optimism being one of them. However, developing qualities requires mastering a range of skills which are diverse and sometimes surprising. For example, to bring more joy and passion into your life, you must be open to experiencing negative emotions. Cultivating such qualities will help you realise your full potential.

B   'The evidence is good that most personality traits can be altered,' says Christopher Peterson, professor of psychology at the University of Michigan, who cites himself as an example. Inherently introverted, he realised early on that as an academic, his reticence would prove disastrous in the lecture hall. So he learned to be more outgoing and to entertain his classes. 'Now my extroverted behaviour is spontaneous,' he says.

C   David Fajgenbaum had to make a similar transition. He was preparing for university, when he had an accident that put an end to his sports career. On campus, he quickly found that beyond ordinary counselling, the university had no services for students who were undergoing physical rehabilitation and suffering from depression like him. He therefore launched a support group to help others in similar situations. He took action despite his own pain – a typical response of an optimist.

D   Suzanne Segerstrom, professor of psychology at the University of Kentucky, believes that the key to increasing optimism is through cultivating optimistic behaviour, rather than positive thinking. She recommends you train yourself to pay attention to good fortune by writing down three positive things that come about each day. This will help you convince yourself that favourable outcomes actually happen all the time, making it easier to begin taking action.

E You can recognise a person who is passionate about a pursuit by the way they are so strongly involved in it. Tanya Streeter's passion is freediving – the sport of plunging deep into the water without tanks or other breathing equipment. Beginning in 1998, she set nine world records and can hold her breath for six minutes. The physical stamina required for this sport is intense but the psychological demands are even more overwhelming. Streeter learned to untangle her fears from her judgment of what her body and mind could do. 'In my career as a competitive freediver, there was a limit to what I could do – but it wasn't anywhere near what I thought it was,' she says.

F Finding a pursuit that excites you can improve anyone's life. The secret about consuming passions, though, according to psychologist Paul Silvia of the University of North Carolina, is that 'they require discipline, hard work and ability, which is why they are so rewarding.' Psychologist Todd Kashdan has this advice for those people taking up a new passion: 'As a newcomer, you also have to tolerate and laugh at your own ignorance. You must be willing to accept the negative feelings that come your way,' he says.

G In 2004, physician-scientist Mauro Zappaterra began his PhD research at Harvard Medical School. Unfortunately, he was miserable as his research wasn't compatible with his curiosity about healing. He finally took a break and during eight months in Santa Fe, Zappaterra learned about alternative healing techniques not taught at Harvard. When he got back, he switched labs to study how cerebrospinal fluid nourishes the developing nervous system. He also vowed to look for the joy in everything, including failure, as this could help him learn about his research and himself.

One thing that can hold joy back is a person's concentration on avoiding failure rather than their looking forward to doing something well. 'Focusing on being safe might get in the way of your reaching your goals,' explains Kashdan. For example, are you hoping to get through a business lunch without embarrassing yourself, or are you thinking about how fascinating the conversation might be?

H Usually, we think of courage in physical terms but ordinary life demands something else. For marketing executive Kenneth Pedeleose, it meant speaking out against something he thought was ethically wrong. The new manager was intimidating staff so Pedeleose carefully recorded each instance of bullying and eventually took the evidence to a senior director, knowing his own job security would be threatened. Eventually the manager was the one to go. According to Cynthia Pury, a psychologist at Clemson University, Pedeleose's story proves the point that courage is not motivated by fearlessness, but by moral obligation. Pury also believes that people can acquire courage. Many of her students said that faced with a risky situation, they first tried to calm themselves down, then looked for a way to mitigate the danger, just as Pedeleose did by documenting his allegations.

Over the long term, picking up a new character trait may help you move toward being the person you want to be. And in the short term, the effort itself could be surprisingly rewarding, a kind of internal adventure.

Questions 14–18

Complete the summary below.

*Choose **NO MORE THAN TWO WORDS** from the passage for each answer.*

Write your answers in boxes 14–18 on your answer sheet.

Psychologists have traditionally believed that a personality **14** .... was impossible and that by a **15** .... , a person's character tends to be fixed. This is not true according to positive psychologists, who say that our personal qualities can be seen as habitual behaviour. One of the easiest qualities to acquire is **16** .... However, regardless of the quality, it is necessary to learn a wide variety of different **17** .... in order for a new quality to develop; for example, a person must understand and feel some **18** .... in order to increase their happiness.

Questions 19–22

Look at the following statements (Questions 19–22) and the list of people below.

*Match each statement with the correct person, **A–G**.*

*Write the correct letter, **A–G**, in boxes 19–22 on your answer sheet.*

19 People must accept that they do not know much when first trying something new.

20 It is important for people to actively notice when good things happen.

21 Courage can be learned once its origins in a sense of responsibility are understood.

22 It is possible to overcome shyness when faced with the need to speak in public.

List of People
A Christopher Peterson
B David Fajgenbaum
C Suzanne Segerstrom
D Tanya Streeter
E Todd Kashdan
F Kenneth Pedeleose
G Cynthia Pury

Questions 23–26

Reading Passage 2 has eight sections, **A–H**.

Which section contains the following information?

*Write the correct letter, **A–H**, in boxes 23–26 on your answer sheet.*

23 a mention of how rational thinking enabled someone to achieve physical goals

24 an account of how someone overcame a sad experience

25 a description of how someone decided to rethink their academic career path

26 an example of how someone risked his career out of a sense of duty

READING PASSAGE 3

*You should spend about 20 minutes on **Questions 27–40**, which are based on Reading Passage 3 below.*

When evolution runs backwards

Evolution isn't supposed to run backwards – yet an increasing number of examples show that it does and that it can sometimes represent the future of a species

The description of any animal as an 'evolutionary throwback' is controversial. For the better part of a century, most biologists have been reluctant to use those words, mindful of a principle of evolution that says 'evolution cannot run backwards'. But as more and more examples come to light and modern genetics enters the scene, that principle is having to be rewritten. Not only are evolutionary throwbacks possible, they sometimes play an important role in the forward march of evolution.

The technical term for an evolutionary throwback is an 'atavism', from the Latin *atavus*, meaning forefather. The word has ugly connotations thanks largely to Cesare Lombroso, a 19th-century Italian medic who argued that criminals were born not made and could be identified by certain physical features that were throwbacks to a primitive, sub-human state.

While Lombroso was measuring criminals, a Belgian palaeontologist called Louis Dollo was studying fossil records and coming to the opposite conclusion. In 1890 he proposed that evolution was irreversible: that 'an organism is unable to return, even partially, to a previous stage already realised in the ranks of its ancestors'. Early 20th-century biologists came to a similar conclusion, though they qualified it

in terms of probability, stating that there is no reason why evolution cannot run backwards – it is just very unlikely. And so the idea of irreversibility in evolution stuck and came to be known as 'Dollo's law'.

If Dollo's law is right, atavisms should occur only very rarely, if at all. Yet almost since the idea took root, exceptions have been cropping up. In 1919, for example, a humpback whale with a pair of leg-like appendages over a metre long, complete with a full set of limb bones, was caught off Vancouver Island in Canada. Explorer Roy Chapman Andrews argued at the time that the whale must be a throwback to a land-living ancestor. 'I can see no other explanation,' he wrote in 1921.

Since then, so many other examples have been discovered that it no longer makes sense to say that evolution is as good as irreversible. And this poses a puzzle: how can characteristics that disappeared millions of years ago suddenly reappear? In 1994, Rudolf Raff and colleagues at Indiana University in the USA decided to use genetics to put a number on the probability of evolution going into reverse. They reasoned that while some evolutionary changes involve the loss of genes and are therefore irreversible, others may be the result of genes being switched off. If these silent genes are somehow switched back on, they argued, long-lost traits could reappear.

Raff's team went on to calculate the likelihood of it happening. Silent genes accumulate random mutations, they reasoned, eventually rendering them useless. So how long can a gene survive in a species if it is no longer used? The team calculated that there is a good chance of silent genes surviving for up to 6 million years in at least a few individuals in a population, and that some might survive as long as 10 million years. In other words, throwbacks are possible, but only to the relatively recent evolutionary past.

As a possible example, the team pointed to the mole salamanders of Mexico and California. Like most amphibians these begin life in a juvenile 'tadpole' state, then metamorphose into the adult form – except for one species, the axolotl, which famously lives its entire life as a juvenile. The simplest explanation for this is that the axolotl lineage alone lost the ability to metamorphose, while others retained it. From a detailed analysis of the salamanders' family tree, however, it is clear that the other lineages evolved from an ancestor that itself had lost the ability to metamorphose. In other words, metamorphosis in mole salamanders is an atavism. The salamander example fits with Raff's 10-million-year time frame.

More recently, however, examples have been reported that break the time limit, suggesting that silent genes may not be the whole story. In a paper published last year, biologist Gunter Wagner of Yale University reported some work on the evolutionary

history of a group of South American lizards called Bachia. Many of these have minuscule limbs; some look more like snakes than lizards and a few have completely lost the toes on their hind limbs. Other species, however, sport up to four toes on their hind legs. The simplest explanation is that the toed lineages never lost their toes, but Wagner begs to differ. According to his analysis of the Bachia family tree, the toed species re-evolved toes from toeless ancestors and, what is more, digit loss and gain has occurred on more than one occasion over tens of millions of years.

So what's going on? One possibility is that these traits are lost and then simply reappear, in much the same way that similar structures can independently arise in unrelated species, such as the dorsal fins of sharks and killer whales. Another more intriguing possibility is that the genetic information needed to make toes somehow survived for tens or perhaps hundreds of millions of years in the lizards and was reactivated. These atavistic traits provided an advantage and spread through the population, effectively reversing evolution.

But if silent genes degrade within 6 to 10 million years, how can long-lost traits be reactivated over longer timescales? The answer may lie in the womb. Early embryos of many species develop ancestral features. Snake embryos, for example, sprout hind limb buds. Later in development these features disappear thanks to developmental programs that say 'lose the leg'. If for any reason this does not happen, the ancestral feature may not disappear, leading to an atavism.

Questions 27–31

*Choose the correct letter, **A**, **B**, **C** or **D**.*

Write the correct letter in boxes 27–31 on your answer sheet.

27 When discussing the theory developed by Louis Dollo, the writer says that

    A   it was immediately referred to as Dollo's law.
    B   it supported the possibility of evolutionary throwbacks.
    C   it was modified by biologists in the early twentieth century.
    D   it was based on many years of research.

28 The humpback whale caught off Vancouver Island is mentioned because of

    A   the exceptional size of its body.
    B   the way it exemplifies Dollo's law.
    C   the amount of local controversy it caused.
    D   the reason given for its unusual features.

29 What is said about 'silent genes'?

    A   Their numbers vary according to species.
    B   Raff disagreed with the use of the term.
    C   They could lead to the re-emergence of certain characteristics.
    D   They can have an unlimited life span.

30 The writer mentions the mole salamander because

    A   it exemplifies what happens in the development of most amphibians.
    B   it suggests that Raff's theory is correct.
    C   it has lost and regained more than one ability.
    D   its ancestors have become the subject of extensive research.

31 Which of the following does Wagner claim?

    A   Members of the Bachia lizard family have lost and regained certain features several times.
    B   Evidence shows that the evolution of the Bachia lizard is due to the environment.
    C   His research into South American lizards supports Raff's assertions.
    D   His findings will apply to other species of South American lizards.

Questions 32–36

*Complete each sentence with the correct ending, **A–G**, below.*

*Write the correct letter, **A–G**, in boxes 32–36 on your answer sheet.*

32   For a long time biologists rejected

33   Opposing views on evolutionary throwbacks are represented by

34   Examples of evolutionary throwbacks have led to

35   The shark and killer whale are mentioned to exemplify

36   One explanation for the findings of Wagner's research is

A	the question of how certain long-lost traits could reappear.
B	the occurrence of a particular feature in different species.
C	parallels drawn between behaviour and appearance.
D	the continued existence of certain genetic information.
E	the doubts felt about evolutionary throwbacks.
F	the possibility of evolution being reversible.
G	Dollo's findings and the convictions held by Lombroso.

Questions 37–40

Do the following statements agree with the claims of the writer in Reading Passage 3?

In boxes 37–40 on your answer sheet, write

YES	if the statement agrees with the claims of the writer
NO	if the statement contradicts the claims of the writer
NOT GIVEN	if it is impossible to say what the writer thinks about this

37   Wagner was the first person to do research on South American lizards.

38   Wagner believes that Bachia lizards with toes had toeless ancestors.

39   The temporary occurrence of long-lost traits in embryos is rare.

40   Evolutionary throwbacks might be caused by developmental problems in the womb.

WRITING

WRITING TASK 1

You should spend about 20 minutes on this task.

> **The diagrams below show the life cycle of a species of large fish called the salmon.**
>
> **Summarise the information by selecting and reporting the main features, and make comparisons where relevant.**

Write at least 150 words.

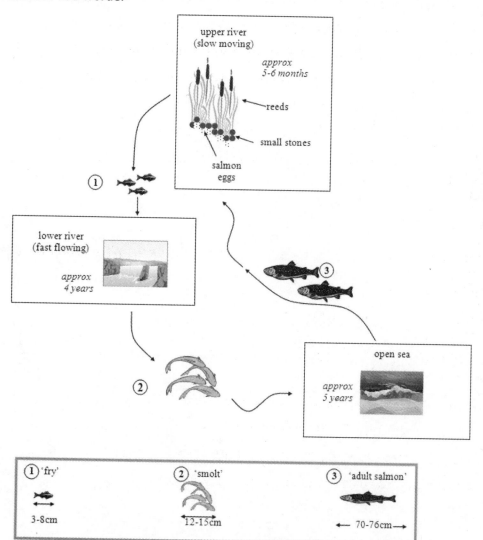

WRITING TASK 2

You should spend about 40 minutes on this task.

Write about the following topic:

> *Many museums charge for admission while others are free.*
>
> *Do you think the advantages of charging people for admission to museums outweigh the disadvantages?*

Give reasons for your answer and include any relevant examples from your own knowledge or experience.

Write at least 250 words.

SPEAKING

PART 1

The examiner asks the candidate about him/herself, his/her home, work or studies and other familiar topics.

EXAMPLE

School

- Did you go to secondary/high school near to where you lived? [Why/Why not?]
- What did you like about your secondary/high school? [Why?]
- Tell me about anything you <u>didn't</u> like at your school.
- How do you think your school could be improved? [Why/Why not?]

PART 2

Describe something you don't have now but would really like to own in the future.

You should say:
> **what this thing is**
> **how long you have wanted to own it**
> **where you first saw it**
and explain why you would like to own it.

You will have to talk about the topic for one to two minutes. You have one minute to think about what you are going to say.
You can make some notes to help you if you wish.

PART 3

Discussion topics:

Owning things

Example questions:
What types of things do young people in your country most want to own today? Why is this?
Why do some people feel they need to own things?
Do you think that owning lots of things makes people happy? Why?

Salaries for skilled people

Example questions:
Do you think television and films can make people want to get new possessions? Why do they have this effect?
Are there any benefits to society of people wanting to get new possessions? Why do you think this is?
Do you think people will consider that having lots of possessions is a sign of success in the future? Why?

General Training Reading and Writing Test A

READING

SECTION 1   Questions 1–14

Read the text below and answer Questions 1–7.

Smoke alarms in the home

Smoke alarms are now a standard feature in Australian homes and are required by the National Building Code in any recently built properties. They are installed to detect the presence of smoke and emit a clear sound to alert you in the event of fire to give you time to escape.

There are two principal types of smoke alarms. Ionization alarms are the cheapest and most readily available smoke alarms. They are also very sensitive to 'flaming fires' – fires that burn fiercely – and will detect them before the smoke gets too thick. However, photoelectric alarms are more effective at detecting slow-burning fires. They are less likely to go off accidentally and so are best for homes with one floor. For the best protection, you should install one of each.

Most battery-powered smoke alarms can be installed by the home owner and do not require professional installation. For the installation of hard-wired smoke alarms, powered from the mains electricity supply, however, you will need the services of a licensed professional. Smoke alarms are usually most effective when located on the ceiling, near or in the middle of the room or hall.

Photoelectric smoke alarms in any quantity may be disposed of in domestic waste. If you have fewer than ten ionization alarms to get rid of, you may put them in your domestic waste. If you have more than ten to dispose of, you should contact your local council.

Your battery-powered smoke alarm will produce a short beep every 60 second to alert you when the battery is running out and needs replacing. Nevertheless, it should be tested every month to ensure that the battery and the alarm sounder are working. Note that the sensitivity in all smoke alarms will reduce over time.

Questions 1–7

Do the following statements agree with the information given in the text on page 104?

In boxes 1–7 on your answer sheet, write

> **TRUE**   *if the statement agrees with the information*
> **FALSE**   *if the statement contradicts the information*
> **NOT GIVEN** *if there is no information on this*

1   All new houses in Australia must have smoke alarms.

2   Photoelectric smoke alarms cost less than ionization smoke alarms.

3   It takes a short time to fit most smoke alarms.

4   Any hard-wired smoke alarm must be fitted by a specialist technician.

5   You should get in touch with your local council before placing any ionisation smoke alarms in household rubbish.

6   Smoke alarms give a warning sound to indicate that battery power is low.

7   Old smoke alarms need to be checked more than once a month.

Read the text below and answer Questions 8–14.

Sydney Opera House Tours

We offer three different tours of this iconic building.

A **The Essential Tour** brings to life the story behind the design and construction of one of the world's most famous landmarks. Using interactive audio-visual technology, your guide will take you on a memorable journey inside the youngest building ever to be World Heritage listed.

B Afterwards, why not stay around and eat at the Studio Café, with its modern Australian menu? Not only can you enjoy the best views in Sydney, you can claim a 20% reduction on the total cost of your meal. (Don't forget to show your ticket in order to claim your discount.)

C Languages: English, French, German

Takes place: Daily between 9am and 5pm

Prices: Adults $35 / Online $29.75

Concessions: Australian seniors and pensioners; students and children of 16 and under $24.50.

Prior bookings are not essential.

D **The Backstage Tour** gives you backstage access to the Sydney Opera House. It is a unique opportunity to experience the real-life dramas behind the stage! You might even get to stand on the concert hall stage, take up a conductor's baton in the orchestra pit and imagine you are leading the performance. You will also get to see inside the stars' dressing rooms. The tour concludes with a complimentary breakfast in the Green Room, the private dining area of performers past and present.

E Takes place: Daily at 7am

Prices: $155. No concessions.

To purchase: Bookings are essential. Limited to 8 people per tour.

Online sales expire at 4.30pm two days prior.

Notes:
The tour includes up to 300 steps.
Flat, rubber-soled shoes must be worn.
For safety reasons, children of 12 years old and under are not permitted.

F **Opera High Tea** consists of a tour where you will walk in the footsteps of world-class singers, dancers and musicians, followed by fine food and music in the spectacular surroundings of the Bennelong Dining Room. What could be better than a treat of delicious light snacks and soft drinks followed by a live recital by a leading Australian singer?
An unforgettable treat for young and old!

G Takes place: Every second Wednesday, 2pm

Duration: 1.5 hours

Prices: $145 per person

Book online or visit the Guided Tours Desk.

Questions 8–14

The text on page 106 has seven sections A–G. Which section mentions the following?

Write the correct letter A–G in boxes 8–14 on your answer sheet.

NB *You may use any letter more than once.*

8   discounts available to younger visitors

9   the need for suitable footwear

10   the opportunity to pretend you are taking part in a concert

11   a restriction on the number of participants

12   a reduction that applies to purchases using the internet

13   the need to book your ticket in advance

14   the length of one of the tours

SECTION 2 *Questions 15–27*

Read the text below and answer Questions 15–21.

USING DIRECT MAIL TO SELL YOUR PRODUCT

When you have set up your own business, you must, of course, start selling your goods or services. One way is by using direct mail – in other words, sending a sales letter (or email) directly to companies that might want to do business with you.

One important factor is your mailing list – that is, who you contact. You can build this up from your own market research, existing clients and advertising responses, or you can contact list brokers and rent or buy a compiled list. If you are contacting a business, it is important to address the letter to the decision maker, ideally by name or at least by job title.

While the desirability and price of the product on offer will obviously influence sales, you also need to gain the maximum impact from your sales letter. To achieve that, bear the following points in mind:

- You have no more than two seconds from when the reader starts the letter to convince them to continue. If you fail, they will throw it away. The opening is crucial to attract their attention. And so that they don't lose interest, avoid having too much text.

- Try to send each mailing in a white envelope. It might be cheaper to use a brown envelope but it doesn't make for such good presentation.

- Include a brochure. Depending on the volume and on whether you can afford the cost, try to use at least two-colour printing for this. If practicable, it may be worth enclosing a free sample – this is a much greater incentive than photographs.

- However interested your potential clients are in buying, they will only do so if it can be done easily. So, include an order form (and of course details of how to return it) with your letter.

- When you receive your replies, assess your response rate and monitor the sales. If necessary, the sales letter can then be amended to attract other clients on subsequent mail shots; make sure each different letter is coded so that monitoring is easy and effective.

- Ensure that each reply is dealt with quickly and professionally. If further details are requested, these must be sent out promptly. There is no point in encouraging potential customers to contact you if your service is slow or non-existent.

Questions 15–21

Complete the sentences below.

*Choose **NO MORE THAN TWO WORDS** from the text for each answer.*

Write your answers in boxes 15–21 on your answer sheet.

15 Sales letters should be sent to the .... in a company.

16 Your letter should make as much .... as possible.

17 The reader's attention needs to be caught by the .... of your letter.

18 Letters should be sent in a ....

19 It is best to print the .... in two or more colours.

20 Consider sending a .... as this is more effective than a picture.

21 You should calculate the .... to your letter.

Read the text below and answer Questions 22–27.

IFCES, the International Federation of Chemical Engineering Societies
Job Specification: Communications Manager

Contract: Permanent (with 3-month probationary period)
Reports to: Chief Executive
Hours: 9:15am – 5:30pm with 1 hour for lunch
Holidays: 23 days per annum + statutory public holidays

Job Summary

To raise the international profile of IFCES. To communicate our objectives, programmes and services to members, the chemical engineering community, the media and the wider public.

Key Responsibilities

- Develop and implement a programme of communications to member associations, the chemical engineering industry, sponsors and the media
- Plan and implement marketing strategies for all IFCES programmes including the World Chemical Engineering Congress
- Write and edit copy for publications intended for internal and external use including *Chemical Engineer Monthly*
- Work with design agencies, web developers and other external contractors to produce high quality corporate and marketing materials
- Research, write and distribute news releases as required, often at short notice and under pressure
- Deal with media enquiries and interview requests. Ensure that good relationships with both mainstream and chemical engineering media are developed and maintained
- Assist in the production of presentations and speeches for board members
- Ensure website content is up to date and consistent
- Develop a consistent corporate identity and ensure its application by all member associations and partner organisations
- Carry out specific duties and projects as directed from time to time

Employee Specification

Essential

- Degree (any discipline)
- Minimum 4 years' experience in a communications role
- Excellent copy writing skills with strong attention to detail, a keen sense of audience and an ability to tailor writing to its particular purpose
- Demonstrable track record of producing high quality corporate publications and marketing materials
- Excellent interpersonal and organisational skills
- Sound IT skills, including working knowledge of Microsoft Office applications
- Willingness to travel internationally

Desirable

- Recognised post-graduate qualification in public relations / journalism / marketing communications
- Knowledge of the global chemical engineering industry and the production of new materials in particular
- Understanding of the concerns surrounding sustainability in chemical engineering
- Ability to speak a foreign language

Questions 22–27

Complete the notes below.

*Choose **NO MORE THAN TWO WORDS** from the text for each answer.*

Write your answers in boxes 22–27 on your answer sheet.

Position: Communications Manager

Summary of role: to improve IFCES's **22** .... around the world

Responsibilities include:

- writing for a number of **23** .... , produced for both IFCES and a wider readership

- producing news releases quickly when necessary

- making sure the **24** .... contains current information.

Employee specification (essential) includes:

- high level skill in writing appropriately
  - for the **25** .... to read
  - to achieve a specific **26** ....
- good IT skills.

Employee specification (desirable) includes:

- relevant qualification at a **27** .... level

- awareness of issues of sustainability in relation to the industry

- knowledge of a foreign language.

SECTION 3   *Questions 28–40*

Read the text on pages 112 and 113 and answer Questions 28–40.

KAURI GUM –
a piece of New Zealand's history

A

The kauri tree is a massive forest tree native to New Zealand. Kauri once formed vast forests over much of the north of the country. Whereas now it is the wood of the kauri which is an important natural resource, in the past it was the tree's sap (the thick liquid which flows inside a tree) which, when hardened into gum, played an important role in New Zealand's early history.

After running from rips or tears in the bark of trees, the sap hardens to form the lumps of gum which eventually fall to the ground and are buried under layers of forest litter. The bark often splits where branches fork from the trunk, and gum accumulates there also.

The early European settlers in New Zealand collected and sold the gum. Gum fresh from the tree was soft and of low value but most of the gum which was harvested had been buried for thousands of years. This gum came in a bewildering variety of colours, degree of transparency and hardness, depending on the length and location of burial, as well as the health of the original tree and the area of the bleeding. Highest quality gum was hard and bright and was usually found at shallow depth on the hills. Lowest quality gum was soft, black or chalky and sugary and was usually found buried in swamps, where it had been in contact with water for a long time. Long periods in the sun or bush fires could transform dull, cloudy lumps into higher quality transparent gum.

B

Virtually all kauri gum was found in the regions of New Zealand where kauri forests grow today – from the middle of the North Island northwards. In Maori and early European times up until 1850, most gum collected was simply picked up from the ground, but, after that, the majority was recovered by digging.

C

The original inhabitants of New Zealand, the Maori, had experimented with kauri gum well before Europeans arrived at the beginning of the nineteenth century. They called it *kapia*, and found it of considerable use.

Fresh gum from trees was prized for its chewing quality, as was buried gum when softened in water and mixed with the juice of a local plant. A piece of gum was often passed around from mouth to mouth when people gathered together until it was all gone, or when they tired of chewing, it was laid aside for future use.

Kauri gum burns readily and was used by Maori people to light fires. Sometimes it was bound in grass, ignited and used as a torch by night fishermen to attract fish.

D

The first kauri gum to be exported from New Zealand was part of a cargo taken back to Australia and England by two early expeditions in 1814 and 1815. By the 1860s, kauri gum's reputation was well established in the overseas markets and European immigrants were joining the Maoris in collecting gum on the hills of northern New Zealand. As the surface gum became more scarce, spades were used to dig up the buried 'treasure'. The increasing number of diggers resulted in rapid growth of the kauri gum exports from 1,000 tons in 1860 to a maximum of over 10,000 tons in 1900.

For fifty years from about 1870 to 1920, the kauri gum industry was a major source of income for settlers in northern New Zealand. As these would-be farmers struggled to break in the land, many turned to gum-digging to earn enough money to support their families and pay for improvements to their farms until better times arrived. By the 1890s, there were 20,000 people engaged in gum-digging. Although many of these, such as farmers, women and children, were only part-time diggers, nearly 7,000 were full-timers. During times of economic difficulty, gum-digging was the only job available where the unemployed from many walks of life could earn a living, if they were prepared to work.

E

The first major commercial use of kauri gum was in the manufacture of high-grade furniture varnish, a kind of clear paint used to treat wood. The best and purest gum that was exported prior to 1910 was used in this way. Kauri gum was used in 70% of the oil varnishes being manufactured in England in the 1890s. It was favoured ahead of other gums because it was easier to process at lower temperatures. The cooler the process could be kept the better, as it meant a paler varnish could be produced.

About 1910, kauri gum was found to be a very suitable ingredient in the production of some kinds of floor coverings such as linoleum. In this way, a use was found for the vast quantities of poorer quality and less pure gum, that had up till then been discarded as waste. Kauri gum's importance in the manufacture of varnish and linoleum was displaced by synthetic alternatives in the 1930s.

F

Fossil kauri gum is rather soft and can be carved easily with a knife or polished with fine sandpaper. In the time of Queen Victoria of England (1837–1901), some pieces were made into fashionable amber beads that women wore around their necks. The occasional lump that contained preserved insects was prized for use in necklaces and bracelets. Many of the gum-diggers enjoyed the occasional spell of carving and produced a wide variety of small sculptured pieces. Many of these carvings can be seen today in local museums.

Over the years, kauri gum has also been used in a number of minor products, such as an ingredient in marine glue and candles. In the last decades it has had a very limited use in the manufacture of extremely high-grade varnish for violins, but the gum of the magnificent kauri tree remains an important part of New Zealand's history.

Questions 28–33

The text has six sections, **A–F**.

Which section contains the following information?

*Write the correct letter, **A–F**, in boxes 28–33 on your answer sheet.*

NB *You may use any letter more than once.*

28 an example of a domestic product made of high-quality gum

29 factors affecting gum quality

30 how kauri gum is formed

31 how gum was gathered

32 the main industrial uses of the gum

33 recent uses of kauri gum

Questions 34–39

Look at the following events in the history of kauri gum in New Zealand (Questions 34–39) and the list of time periods below.

*Match each event with the correct time period, **A–I**.*

*Write the correct letter, **A–I**, in boxes 34–39 on your answer sheet.*

34   Kauri gum was first used in New Zealand.

35   The amount of kauri gum sent overseas peaked.

36   The collection of kauri gum supplemented farmers' incomes.

37   Kauri gum was made into jewellery.

38   Kauri gum was used in the production of string instruments.

39   Most of the kauri gum was found underground.

List of Time Periods

A before the 1800s		**B** in 1900	
C in 1910		**D** between the late 1800s and the early 1900s	
E between the 1830s and 1900		**F** in 1814 and 1815	
G after 1850		**H** in the 1930s	
I in recent times			

Question 40

*Choose the correct letter, **A, B, C** or **D**.*

Write the correct letter in box 40 on your answer sheet.

40   What was most likely to reduce the quality of kauri gum?

    A   how long it was buried
    B   exposure to water
    C   how deep it was buried
    D   exposure to heat

WRITING

WRITING TASK 1

You should spend about 20 minutes on this task.

> *You are going to another country to study. You would like to do a part-time job while you are studying, so you want to ask a friend who lives there for some help.*
>
> *Write a letter to this friend. In your letter*
> * *give details of your study plans*
> * *explain why you want to get a part-time job*
> * *suggest how your friend could help you find a job*

Write at least 150 words.

You do **NOT** need to write any addresses.

Begin your letter as follows:

Dear .... ,

WRITING TASK 2

You should spend about 40 minutes on this task.

Write about the following topic:

> *In many countries, the amount of crime is increasing.*
>
> *What do you think are the main causes of crime?*
>
> *How can we deal with those causes?*

Give reasons for your answer and include any relevant examples from your own knowledge or experience.

Write at least 250 words.

General Training Reading and Writing Test B

SECTION 1   *Questions 1–14*

Read the text below and answer Questions 1–7.

PASSPORT APPLICATION

You will need to fill in an application for a passport in the following circumstances: if you are applying for a passport for the first time, if you wish to replace your current passport, if your passport has expired, or if it has been lost or stolen. Your application form must be completed in your own handwriting.

As proof of your citizenship and identity, you must enclose either your passport or your birth certificate. All documents must be originals; these will be returned with your passport.

The standard time to process an application is up to 10 working days. The processing begins from when we have received the completed application form. Applicants should expect delays if the Passport Office receives a form with missing information. Extra time should be allowed for delivery to and from the Passport Office.

Please provide two identical passport photos of yourself. Both photos must be the same in all respects and must be less than 12 months old.

Ask someone who can identify you to fill in the 'Proof of Identity' information and identify one of your photos. This person will be called your witness and needs to meet the following requirements: a witness must be aged 16 years or over, be contactable by phone during normal office hours and be the holder of a valid passport. A witness should fill in the 'Proof of Identity' page in their own handwriting. A witness must also write the full name of the person applying for the passport on the back of one of the photos, sign their own name and date the back of the same photo. Photos with this identifying information written in the applicant's own handwriting will not be accepted.

Questions 1–7

Do the following statements agree with the information given in the text on page 117?

In boxes 1–7 on your answer sheet, write

> **TRUE**   *if the statement agrees with the information*
> **FALSE**   *if the statement contradicts the information*
> **NOT GIVEN** *if there is no information on this*

1   A husband can fill in an application form for his wife. *Not given*

2   Photocopies of documents are acceptable in some circumstances. *Not given*

3   An incomplete application will affect processing time. *True*

4   The passport photos included with your application must be in colour. *Not given*

5   A witness can be a relative of the applicant. *Not given*

6   Anyone acting as a witness must have a passport. *True*

7   The passport applicant must sign their name on the back of both photos. *True*

Questions 8–14

The text on page 120 has seven sections, **A–G**.

Choose the correct heading for each section from the list of headings below.

*Write the correct number, **i–x**, in boxes 8–14 on your answer sheet.*

List of Headings
i   Departure procedures
ii   Observation area
iii Baggage services
iv   Meeting facilities
v   Healthcare services
vi   Flight information
vii Currency exchange
viii Health and safety advice
ix   Departure fees
x   Tourist travel centre

8   Section **A**

9   Section **B**

10   Section **C**

11   Section **D**

12   Section **E**

13   Section **F**

14   Section **G**

Auckland International Airport Services

A The second floor of the international terminal offers a view of the airfield and all incoming and outgoing flights. There is a café situated here as well as a restaurant, which is available for all airport visitors to use.

B We are open for all international flights and provide a comprehensive service for visitors to the city. Brochures on a range of attractions are available, and we also offer a booking service for accommodation and transport. Shuttle buses into the city centre are provided at a competitive price.

C Passengers who require urgent medical attention should dial 9877 on any public telephone in the terminal. The airport pharmacy is located on the ground floor near the departure lounge, and stocks a comprehensive range of products.

D Departing passengers can completely seal their luggage or packages in recyclable polythene to protect them from damage. Luggage storage, charged at $10 per hour, is available on the first floor. Transit passengers have free access to storage facilities.

E Every international passenger, with the exception of children under 12 years of age and transit passengers in Auckland for less than 24 hours, is required to make a payment of $25 when leaving the country. This can be arranged at the National Bank on the ground floor.

F As Auckland International Airport has adopted the 'quiet airport' concept, there are usually no announcements made over the public address system. Details of all arrivals and departures are displayed on the monitors located in the terminal halls and lounge areas.

G The airport caters for the needs of business travellers and has several rooms available for seminars or business gatherings. These are located adjacent to the airport medical centre on the first floor. For information and bookings please contact the Airport Business Manager on extension 5294.

SECTION 2   *Questions 15–27*

Read the text below and answer Questions 15–20.

Shooting Star is an organisation which offers special training for school leavers.

 # Planning a Gap Year

The best reason to take a gap year between school and work or higher education is to improve your CV with experience overseas. This is why some school leavers in Britain now consider a year out to be essential. Many want to travel, with Sydney the favourite destination. Shooting Star is an organisation that helps school leavers by offering training followed by appropriate employment.

We at Shooting Star offer much more than a trip abroad. At Shooting Star you acquire skills that lead to interesting jobs both for your gap year and future holidays. Magazines are full of 'Wanted' adverts for washing up in a restaurant. Well, we don't do that – it's not our idea of excitement. We offer school leavers the chance for outdoor adventure, to teach things like sailing and snowboarding. No choice, really! In your year out you train, travel and work; you can combine work with pleasure and reap the rewards. You could become an experienced yacht skipper or instructor and many people go on to spend their future holidays being paid to enjoy their favourite sport.

Australians and New Zealanders travel to Europe and North America in large numbers to gain overseas experience. Those who qualify with Shooting Star are very soon using their skills in jobs they could only dream about before, working outdoors and seeing more of the world. Wherever you come from, a gap year with Shooting Star means professional training and international adventure.

Top tips for a successful gap year:
☆ Design your gap year in outline before applying for a permanent job or a college place. Human Resources officers or Admissions tutors will be impressed by a thought-out plan.
☆ What's more important to you – travel or work experience? You can be flexible with travel plans but you must research job opportunities in advance. Go to our website and click on Recruitment for ideas.
☆ Who do you know who has taken a gap year before? Shooting Star can put you in touch with someone who has just completed one.
☆ Sort out the admin in plenty of time – air tickets, visas, insurance and medical matters such as vaccinations for some destinations. These are your responsibility.
☆ Who is in charge of your affairs while you are away? There will be forms to fill and letters to answer.
☆ Allow plenty of time to settle back home on your return – and don't be surprised if it takes some time to readjust to everyday life!

Questions 15–20

Do the following statements agree with the information given in the text on page 121?

In boxes 15–20 on your answer sheet, write

> **TRUE**　　　 *if the statement agrees with the information*
> **FALSE**　　　*if the statement contradicts the information*
> **NOT GIVEN**　*if there is no information on this*

15　For some young British people, the purpose of a gap year is to improve their academic qualifications.

16　Shooting Star finds employment for young people in the catering industry.

17　Training with Shooting Star can be expensive.

18　New trainees find it easy to get the sort of work they want.

19　New trainees who want work experience should check out vacancies before they depart.

20　Shooting Star helps with travel arrangements.

Questions 21–27

Read the text below and answer Questions 21–27.

Succeeding at Interviews

A Getting invited to an interview means you have passed the first hurdle – your application must have made a good impression. Now you need to prepare yourself for the interview to make sure you make the most of this opportunity. There are a number of things you can do.

B Firstly you can do some research. Find out about the employer and the job, ask for an information pack or speak to people you know who work for the company. Try to plan for the interview by asking who will be interviewing you and whether there will be a test to take.

C Prepare for questions you might be asked. Some common ones are the reason why you want the job, whether you have done this kind of work before, what your strengths and weaknesses are, and which leisure pursuits you enjoy.

D Another important point is never to run the risk of arriving late. For example, consider making a 'dummy run' in advance to see how long the journey will take. Check out public transport or, if you are going by car, the nearest parking. Aim to arrive about 10 minutes before the interview is due to start.

E It is also crucial to give plenty of thought to what you are going to wear. This will depend on the job you are going for. There is no need to buy a new outfit, but aim to look neat and tidy. Remember, if you look good it will help you feel good.

F You need to make a good impression. Interviews can vary from a relatively informal 'one-to-one' chat to a very formal panel situation. Whatever the circumstances, you will give yourself an advantage by being friendly and polite, by making eye contact with the interviewer and by selling yourself by focusing on your strengths.

G There are also things you should avoid doing at your interview. First of all, don't exaggerate. For example, if you don't have the exact experience the employer is looking for, say so and explain you are willing to learn. Don't simply give 'yes' and 'no' answers, but answer questions as fully as you can. And lastly don't forget to ask questions as well as answering them.

H One final thing to remember: it is important to show good team spirit, that you possess good people skills and that you are friendly and approachable. Finally, remember to be enthusiastic and show that you can be flexible.

Questions 21–27

The text on page 123 has eight sections, **A–H**.

Which section mentions the following?

*Write the correct letter, **A–H**, in boxes 21–27 on your answer sheet.*

NB *You may use any letter more than once.*

21   the importance of good manners A

22   using your contacts F

23   giving adequate responses C

24   getting on well with colleagues B H

25   the information you may need to provide B

26   being honest with the interviewer C

27   being punctual D

SECTION 3   *Questions 28–40*

Read the text on pages 125 and 126 and answer Questions 28–40.

Serendipity – accidental discoveries in science

What do photography, dynamite, insulin and artificial sweetener have in common? Serendipity! These diverse discoveries, which have made our everyday living more convenient, were discovered partly by chance. However, Louis Pasteur noted the additional requirement involved in serendipity when he said, '… chance favours only the prepared mind'.

The discovery of modern photography provides an example of serendipity. In 1838, L. J. M. Daguerre was attempting to 'fix' images onto a copper photographic plate. After adding a silver coating to the plate and exposing it to iodine vapour, he found that the photographic image was improved but still very weak. Desperate after an investigation lasting several months, Daguerre placed a lightly exposed photographic plate in the cupboard in which laboratory chemicals such as alcohol and collodion were stored. To his amazement, when he removed the plate several days later, Daguerre found a strong image on its surface.

This image had been created by chance. It was at this point that Louis Pasteur's 'additional requirement' came into play: Daguerre's training told him that one or more of the chemicals in the cupboard was responsible for intensifying the image. After a break of two weeks, Daguerre systematically placed new photographic plates in the cupboard, removing one chemical each day. Unpredictably, good photographic images were created even after all chemicals had been removed. Daguerre then noticed that some mercury had spilled onto the cupboard shelf, and he concluded that the mercury vapour must have improved the photographic result. From this discovery came the universal adoption of the silver-mercury process to develop photographs.

Daguerre's serendipitous research effort was rewarded, a year later, with a medal conferred by the French government. Many great scientists have benefited from serendipity, including Nobel Prize winners. In fact the scientist who established the Nobel Prize was himself blessed with serendipity. In 1861, the Nobel family built a factory in Stockholm to produce nitroglycerine, a colourless and highly explosive oil that had first been prepared by an Italian chemist fifteen years earlier. Nitroglycerine was known to be volatile and unpredictable, often exploding as a result of very small knocks. But the Nobel family believed that this new explosive could solve a major problem facing the Swedish State Railways – the need to dig channels and tunnels through mountains so that the developing railway system could expand.

However, as turnover increased, so did the number of accidental explosions resulting from the use of nitroglycerine. Some people blamed the people who used the explosive more than the substance itself, because nitroglycerine had become popular for inappropriate purposes such as polishing the leather of shoes.

At the age of thirty, Alfred Nobel made the first of his major inventions: an innovative blasting cap, a device designed to control the nitroglycerine explosion. Nobel was also determined to discover a way to make this explosive safer to manufacture, transport and use. Firstly, he experimented with adding chemicals to nitroglycerine, but because the chemicals required huge amounts of resources and energy to wash out, this process was considered to be impractical. He then tried to use fibrous material such as sawdust, charcoal or paper to stabilise the explosive, but these combustible materials tended to catch fire when placed near nitroglycerine. As an alternative, he added powdered brick dust to tame the explosive, as he knew that brick dust would not catch fire. However, the brick dust reduced the explosive power of the product, and so was also found to be unsatisfactory.

According to one version of how the eventual solution was found, a metal container of nitroglycerine sprang a leak, and some of the liquid soaked into packaging material that lay around the container. Nobel immediately set to work to examine the connection between the two materials and found that when the packaging material was mixed with nitroglycerine it could be pressed into a compact solid. This solid retained the explosive power of the liquid, but was entirely safe and reliable because it would not ignite until set off by a blasting cap.

As a scientist who had worked systematically towards a solution for a number of years, Nobel immediately understood the importance of this discovery. But the discovery had only come about because of his perseverance. Through Nobel's clear vision, systematic research and his quick grasp of the significance of his discovery, he set himself apart from the many scientists who were not 'fortunate' enough to create new products that would make them famous.

Alfred Nobel, a lifelong pacifist, hoped that his explosive would be a powerful deterrent to warfare. Nobel sought to achieve permanent worldwide peace. In setting up the Nobel Foundation and the Nobel Peace Prizes, he hoped to accomplish what he had not been able to do during his lifetime: to encourage research and activities that would bestow the 'greatest benefit to mankind', especially peace and fraternity between nations. His vision was of a peaceful world.

Questions 28–31

Complete each sentence with the correct ending, **A–G**, below.

Write the correct letter, **A–G**, in boxes 28–31 on your answer sheet.

28 Nobel found that adding chemicals

29 Nobel found that adding sawdust and paper

30 Nobel found that adding brick dust

31 Nobel found that mixing nitroglycerine with packaging

A	decreased the energy of the explosion.	**E**	made the process safer.
B	lengthened the time required.	**F**	increased the flammability of the mixture.
C	made the process unworkable.	**G**	resulted in lower reliability.
D	reduced the manufacturing costs.		

Questions 32–37

Look at the following statements (Questions 32–37) and the list of options below.

Match each statement with the correct option, **A**, **B** or **C**.

Write the correct letter, **A**, **B** or **C**, in boxes 32–37 on your answer sheet.

NB You may use any letter more than once.

32 He recognised the significance of an unexpected result.

33 He depended on the help of colleagues to solve a problem.

34 He used different methods to find a solution to the problem.

35 He was encouraged to do this research by his government.

36 He received an award in recognition of his scientific work.

37 He worked for a long time to find a way of keeping a process under control.

List of Options

A true of both Daguerre and Nobel
B true of neither Daguerre nor Nobel
C true of only one of them

Questions 38–40

Complete the summary below.

*Choose **NO MORE THAN TWO WORDS** from the text for each answer.*

Write your answers in boxes 38–40 on your answer sheet.

Daguerre's Experiments

Daguerre's work illustrated the comment made by Louis Pasteur that in order to take full advantage of a lucky discovery, scientists need to have a **38** .... He found that exposure to **39** .... had the desired effect on a silver-coated photographic plate, but only to a very limited extent. To his great surprise the image then became much clearer when it was stored in a cupboard. By a process of elimination, he discovered that collodion and alcohol were not responsible for this improvement. In fact, the removal of all the **40** .... did not affect the quality of the image. It was some spilt mercury that had produced the effect.

WRITING

WRITING TASK 1

You should spend about 20 minutes on this task.

You and some friends ate a meal at a restaurant to celebrate a special occasion, and you were very pleased with the food and service.

Write a letter to the restaurant manager. In your letter
- *give details of your visit to the restaurant*
- *explain the reason for the celebration*
- *say what was good about the food and the service*

Write at least 150 words.

You do **NOT** need to write any addresses.

Begin your letter as follows:

Dear Sir or Madam,

WRITING TASK 2

You should spend about 40 minutes on this task.

Write about the following topic:

Some parents buy their children a large number of toys to play with.

What are the advantages and disadvantages for the child of having a large number of toys?

Give reasons for your answer and include any relevant examples from your own knowledge or experience.

Write at least 250 words.

Audioscripts

SECTION 1

TRAVEL AGENT:	Good morning. World Tours. My name is Jamie. How can I help you?
ANDREA:	Good morning. I want some information on self-drive tours in the USA. Could you send me a brochure?
TRAVEL AGENT:	Of course. Could I have your name please?
ANDREA:	Andrea <u>Brown</u>.
TRAVEL AGENT:	Thank you. And your address?
ANDREA:	24, <u>Ardleigh</u> Road.
TRAVEL AGENT:	Can you spell that?
ANDREA:	A-R-D-L-E-I-G-H Road.
TRAVEL AGENT:	Postcode?
ANDREA:	BH5 2OP
TRAVEL AGENT:	Thanks. And can I have your phone number?
ANDREA:	Is a mobile alright?
TRAVEL AGENT:	Fine.
ANDREA:	It's 07786643091.
TRAVEL AGENT:	Thank you. And can I ask you where you heard about World Tours? From a friend? Or did you see an advert somewhere?
ANDREA:	No, I read about you in the <u>newspaper</u>.
TRAVEL AGENT:	OK, I'll get the brochures in the post to you but can I give you some information over the phone. What kinds of things do you want to do on your holiday?
ANDREA:	I'm interested in going to California with my family. I've got two children and we want to hire a car.
TRAVEL AGENT:	OK. We have a couple of self-drive tours there visiting different places of interest in California. The first one begins in Los Angeles and there's plenty of time to visit some of the <u>theme</u> parks there.
ANDREA:	That's something on my children's list so I'd want to include that.
TRAVEL AGENT:	Good. Then you drive to San Francisco. From San Francisco you can drive to Yosemite Park where you spend a couple of nights. You can choose to stay in a lodge or on the campsite.
ANDREA:	I don't like the idea of staying in a <u>tent</u>. It'd be too hot.
TRAVEL AGENT:	Right. And the tour ends in Las Vegas.
ANDREA:	OK.
TRAVEL AGENT:	The other trip we can arrange is slightly different. It starts in San Francisco. Then you drive south to Cambria.
ANDREA:	Someone told me there's a really nice <u>castle</u> near Cambria. Will we go near that?
TRAVEL AGENT:	Hearst Castle is on that road so you could stop there.
ANDREA:	Good. I'd like to do that. Does this trip also go into the desert?
TRAVEL AGENT:	No, it continues to Santa Monica where most people like to stop and do some shopping.
ANDREA:	We have enough of that at home so that doesn't interest us.

Example appears beside "Andrea Brown."

Q1 appears beside "24, Ardleigh Road."

Q2 appears beside "No, I read about you in the newspaper."

Q3 appears beside "plenty of time to visit some of the theme parks there."

Q4 appears beside "I don't like the idea of staying in a tent. It'd be too hot."

Q5 appears beside "Someone told me there's a really nice castle near Cambria. Will we go near that?"

TRAVEL AGENT:	OK. Well you could go straight on to San Diego.	
ANDREA:	That's good for <u>beaches</u> isn't it?	*Q6*
TRAVEL AGENT:	That's right, that's a good place to relax and your children might like to visit the zoo before flying home.	
ANDREA:	I don't think so. We want some time for sunbathing and swimming.	

ANDREA:	So how many days are the trips and how much do they cost?	
TRAVEL AGENT:	The first one I told you about is a self-drive tour through California which lasts twelve days and covers <u>2,020</u> kilometres. The shortest journey is 206 km and the longest is 632 kilometres. The cost is £525 per person. That includes accommodation, car rental and a <u>flight</u> but no meals.	*Q7* *Q8*
ANDREA:	OK. And the other trip?	
TRAVEL AGENT:	That lasts nine days but you spend only three days on the road. You cover about 980 kilometres altogether.	
ANDREA:	So is that cheaper then?	
TRAVEL AGENT:	Yes, it's almost a hundred pounds cheaper. It's £<u>429</u> per person, which is a good deal.	*Q9*
ANDREA:	So that covers accommodation and car hire. What about flights?	
TRAVEL AGENT:	They aren't included. But these hotels offer <u>dinner</u> in the price.	*Q10*
ANDREA:	OK. Well, thank you very much. I'll be in touch when I've had a chance to look at the brochure.	
TRAVEL AGENT:	I'm pleased to help. Goodbye.	
ANDREA:	Goodbye.	

SECTION 2

On behalf of LP Clubs, I'd like to welcome you all here today. My name's Sandy Fisher and I'm one of the fitness managers here. Before we start our tour of the club I'll just run through some basic information about the facilities we have here, including recent improvements, and explain the types of membership available.

Our greatest asset is probably our <u>swimming pool which at 25 metres isn't Olympic-sized, but now we've expanded it to eight lanes, it's much wider</u>. This means there are rarely more than a couple of people at a time in each lane. Unfortunately, there isn't space for an outdoor pool here but the glass roof on the swimming pool is partly retractable, which means you can enjoy something of the open-air experience on warmer days.   *Q11 & 12*

Our <u>recently refurbished fitness suite</u> has all the latest exercise equipment including ten new running machines, and a wide range of weight-training machines. Each member is given full training in how to operate the equipment and there is always a trainer on duty to offer help and advice. Although we do have adult-only times after 6 and at certain times at weekends, children are well catered for. Older children continue to benefit from a wide range of tuition; anything from trampolining to yoga.   *Q11 & 12*

One thing all our members appreciate about us is that we take very good care of them. This starts on day one with your personal assessment. You are asked to fill in a questionnaire <u>giving details of any health problems</u>. One of our personal trainers will then go through this with you.   *Q13*

The trainer will then <u>take you through the safety rules</u> for using the equipment in the fitness suite. During your next exercise session a personal trainer will work with you to make sure you understand these. It's very important to do this because we really do want to avoid   *Q14* having any sports injuries. There's a lot more to looking after yourself than simply lifting weights!

At the end of the personal assessment, <u>the trainer will draw up a plan, outlining what you</u> <u>should try to achieve within a six-week period</u>. This will then be reviewed at the end of the six weeks. *Q15*

Now, I'll just quickly run through the types of membership we have available. <u>All members</u> <u>must pay a joining fee of £90</u> in addition to the rates for the monthly membership fees. <u>Gold membership entitles you to free entry at all LP Clubs.</u> There are now LP clubs in all major cities and towns so if you travel a lot this will be a great advantage. Individual gold membership costs £50 a month and joint membership for you and your partner will cost £75. *Q16* *Q17*

Premier membership is for professional people whose work commitments make it difficult for them to use the club during the day and so <u>LP gives booking preferences to Premier</u> <u>members at peak times</u>. This means you will find it easier to book the sessions at times that suit you. Reciprocal arrangements with other LP Clubs are available to Premier members. Premier membership is for individuals only, but <u>you will be sent passes for</u> <u>guests every month</u>. The monthly fee is £65. *Q18* *Q19*

You don't have to have any special clothes or equipment when you visit the club. We provide robes and hairdryers in the changing rooms, but <u>it's very important to remember</u> <u>your photo card</u> because you won't be able to get in without it. *Q20*

For people who aren't working during the day then …

SECTION 3

JOHN:	Erm … hello Professor, I'm John Wishart. I'm working on my entry for the Global Design Competition. My tutor said you might be able to help me with it.
PROFESSOR:	Ah, yes, I got a copy of your drawings. Come in and tell me about it. What sort of competition is it?
JOHN:	Well, it's an international design competition and <u>we have to come up with</u> <u>a new design for a typical domestic kitchen appliance</u>. *Q21*
PROFESSOR:	I see, and are there any special conditions? Does it have to save energy for example?
JOHN:	Actually that was the focus in last year's competition. This year's different. We have to adopt an innovative approach to existing technology, using it in a way that hasn't been thought of before.
PROFESSOR:	I see, that sounds tricky. And what kitchen appliance have you chosen?
JOHN:	Well, I decided to choose the dishwasher.
PROFESSOR:	Interesting, what made you choose that?
JOHN:	Well, they're an everyday kitchen appliance in most Australian houses but they're all pretty boring and almost identical to each other. <u>I think</u> <u>some people will be prepared to pay a little extra for something that looks</u> <u>different</u>. *Q22*
PROFESSOR:	That's a nice idea. I see you've called your design 'the Rockpool'; why is that?
JOHN:	Basically because it looks like the rock pools you find on a beach. The top is made of glass so that you can look down into it.
PROFESSOR:	And there's a stone at the bottom. Is that just for decoration?

JOHN:	Actually it does have a function. <u>Instead of pushing a button, you turn the stone.</u>	Q23
PROFESSOR:	So it's really just a novel way of starting the dishwasher.	
JOHN:	That's right.	
PROFESSOR:	It's a really nice design, but what makes it innovative?	
JOHN:	Well, I decided to make a dishwasher that uses carbon dioxide.	
PROFESSOR:	In place of water and detergent? How will you manage that?	
JOHN:	The idea is to pressurise the carbon dioxide so that it becomes a liquid. The fluid is then released into the dishwasher where it cleans the dishes all by itself.	
PROFESSOR:	Sounds like a brilliant idea! Your system will totally do away with the need for strong detergents. So what happens once the dishes are clean?	
JOHN:	Well, to allow them to dry, the liquid carbon dioxide and the waste materials all go to an area called the holding chamber. <u>That's where the liquid is depressurised and so it reverts to a gas.</u> Then the oil and grease are separated out and sent to the waste system.	Q24
PROFESSOR:	It sounds like you've thought it all out very thoroughly. So, what happens to the carbon dioxide once the process is complete? Not wasted I hope.	
JOHN:	Actually, that's where the real savings are made. <u>The carbon dioxide is sent back to the cylinder and can be used again and again.</u>	Q25
PROFESSOR:	What a terrific idea. Do you think it will ever be built?	
JOHN:	Probably not, but that's OK.	
PROFESSOR:	Well, I'm sure a lot of positive things will come out of your design.	

PROFESSOR:	Now, you seem to have thought about everything so what exactly did you need me to help you with?	
JOHN:	Well, my design has made it to the final stage of the competition and, <u>in a few months' time, I have to give a presentation, and that's the part I was hoping you could help me with.</u>	Q26
PROFESSOR:	Right, well that should be easy enough. What have you managed to do so far?	
JOHN:	Well, I've got detailed drawings to show how it will work and I've also written a 500-word paper on it.	
PROFESSOR:	I see. Well, <u>if you want to stand a good chance of winning you really need a model of the machine.</u>	Q27
JOHN:	Yes, I thought I might but I'm having a few problems.	
PROFESSOR:	What is the main difficulty so far? Let me guess – is it the materials?	
JOHN:	<u>Yes. I want it to look professional but everything that's top quality is also very expensive.</u>	Q28
PROFESSOR:	Look, projects like this are very important to us. They really help lift our profile. <u>So why don't you talk to the university about a grant?</u> I can help you fill out the application forms if you like.	Q29
JOHN:	That would be great.	
PROFESSOR:	<u>You'd better show me this paper you've written as well. For a global competition such as this you need to make sure the technical details you've given are accurate and thorough.</u>	Q30
JOHN:	That would be a great help.	
PROFESSOR:	Is there anything else I can do?	
JOHN:	Well, I'm really …	

SECTION 4

Today we continue our series on ecology and conservation with a look at a particularly endangered member of the black bear family. <u>One in ten black bears is actually born with a white coat, which is the result of a special gene that surfaces in a few</u>. Local people have named it 'the spirit bear'. And <u>according to the legends of these communities, its snowy fur brings with it a special power.</u> Because of this, it has always been highly regarded by them – so much that they do not speak of seeing it to anyone else. <u>It is their way of protecting it when strangers visit the area.</u>   Q31 Q32 Q33

The white bear's habitat is quite interesting. The bear's strong relationship with the old-growth rainforest is a complex one. The white bear relies on the huge centuries-old trees in the forest in many ways. For example, <u>the old-growth trees have extremely long roots that help prevent erosion of the soil along the banks of the many fish streams</u>. Keeping these banks intact is important because these streams are home to salmon, which are the bear's main food source. In return, the bear's feeding habits nurture the forest. As the bears eat the salmon, they discard the skin and bones in great amounts on the forest floor, which provide vital nutrients. These produce lush vegetation that sustains thousands of other types of life forms, from birds to insects and more.   Q34

<u>Today, the spirit bear lives off the coast of the province of British Columbia on a few islands</u>. There is great concern for their survival since it is estimated that less than two hundred of these white bears remain. The best way to protect them is to make every effort to preserve the delicate balance of their forest environment – in other words, their ecosystem.   Q35

The greatest threat to the bear's existence is the loss of its habitat. Over many years, logging companies have stripped the land by cutting down a large number of trees. In addition, <u>they have built roads which have fractured the areas where the bear usually feeds, and many hibernation sites have also been lost</u>. The logging of the trees along the streams has damaged the places where the bears fish. To make matters worse, <u>the number of salmon in those streams is declining because there is no legal limit on fishing at the moment.</u>   Q36 Q37

All these influences have a negative impact on the spirit bear's very existence, <u>which is made all the more fragile by the fact that reproduction among these bears has always been disappointingly low.</u>   Q38

And so, what's the situation going forward? Community organizations, environmental groups and the British Columbia government are now working together on the problem. <u>The government is now requiring logging companies to adopt a better logging method,</u> which is a positive step. However, these measures alone may not be sufficient to ensure a healthy population of the spirit bear in the future.   Q39

Other steps also need to be taken. While it is important to maintain the spirit bear's habitat, <u>there also needs to be more emphasis on its expansion</u>. The move is justified as it will also create space for other bears that are losing their homes …   Q40

TEST 2

SECTION 1

INTERVIEWER:	Excuse me.
LUISA:	Yes?
INTERVIEWER:	I wonder if you could spare a few minutes to do a survey on transport. It won't take long.
LUISA:	No, that's fine.
INTERVIEWER:	Lovely. The survey is on behalf of the local council. They'd like to know about what transport you use and any suggestions for improvement. Can I start by asking you how you travelled to town today?
LUISA:	Sure. I came on the <u>bus</u>.	*Example*
INTERVIEWER:	Great. Now can I get a few details about yourself?
LUISA:	OK.
INTERVIEWER:	What's your name?
LUISA:	It's Luisa ….
INTERVIEWER:	Yes.
LUISA:	<u>Hardie</u>.	Q1
INTERVIEWER:	Can you spell that, please?
LUISA:	Yes, it's H-A-R-D-I-E.
INTERVIEWER:	Great. Thanks. And can I have your address?
LUISA:	It's <u>19</u>, White Stone Road.	Q2
INTERVIEWER:	Oh, right. I know that area. It's Bradfield, isn't it?
LUISA:	That's right.
INTERVIEWER:	Is the postcode GT7?
LUISA:	It's actually <u>G-T-8, 2-L-C</u>.	Q3
INTERVIEWER:	Great. And could I ask what your job is? Are you a student?
LUISA:	I've actually just finished my training. <u>I'm a hairdresser</u>.	Q4
INTERVIEWER:	Oh, right. And one more question in this section. What is the reason for you coming into town today?
LUISA:	Actually it's not for shopping today, which would be my normal reason, but <u>to see the dentist</u>.	Q5
INTERVIEWER:	Right. Thanks.

INTERVIEWER:	Now in this last section I'd like you to give us some ideas about the facilities and arrangements in the city for getting to and from work, er, any suggestions you have for improvements.
LUISA:	Well, something I've thought about for some time is that when I do walk and I'm doing a later shift, I think <u>the lighting should be better</u>.	Q6
INTERVIEWER:	Yes, good point.
LUISA:	And of course, I think it's a real shame they've been cutting down on the number of footpaths. They should have more of those. Then people would walk more.
INTERVIEWER:	Yes, right.
LUISA:	And, <u>I don't think there are enough trains. That's why I don't use them – you have to wait so long</u>.	Q7
INTERVIEWER:	Thanks. And finally I'd like to ask your opinion on cycling. As you may know, there's a drive in the city to get more people to cycle to work.

LUISA:	Right.	
INTERVIEWER:	But we realise that there are things which the council, but also employers, might do to help encourage workers to cycle to work.	
LUISA:	Yep. Well, I have thought about it and where I work <u>there are no safe places to leave your bikes</u>.	*Q8*
INTERVIEWER:	OK.	
LUISA:	And also, I'd have to cycle uphill and on a hot day I'd arrive at work pretty sweaty so <u>I think I'd need a shower somewhere at work</u>.	*Q9*
INTERVIEWER:	Right.	
LUISA:	And I suppose the last thing is that <u>I wouldn't be all that confident about cycling on such busy roads. I think I'd like to see you offering training for that</u>, you know, I'd feel a lot better about starting if that was the case.	*Q10*
INTERVIEWER:	Well, that's very helpful. Thank you very much for your time.	
LUISA:	No problem. Bye.	

SECTION 2

Good morning. I'm very pleased to have this opportunity to say a little about two exciting new developments in the city: the Brackenside Open-Air Swimming Pool and the children's Adventure Playground in Central Park. As many of you may know, <u>the idea for these</u> *Q11* <u>initiatives came from you, the public</u>, in the extensive consultation exercise which the City Council conducted last year. And they have been realised using money from the SWRDC – the South West Regional Development Commission.

First of all, Brackenside Pool. As many of the older members of the audience will remember, there used to be a wonderful open-air pool on the sea front 30 years ago but it had to close when it was judged to be unsafe. For the design of this new heated pool, we were very happy to secure the talents of internationally renowned architect Ellen Wendon, who has managed to combine a charming 1930s design, which fits in so well with many of the other buildings in the area, with up-to-the-minute features <u>such as a recycling system –</u> *Q12* <u>the only one of its kind in the world – which enables seawater to be used in the pool</u>.

Now, <u>there has been quite a bit of discussion in the local press about whether there</u> *Q13* <u>would be enough room for the number of visitors we're hoping to attract</u>, but the design is deceptive and there have been rigorous checks about capacity. Also, just in case you were wondering, we're on schedule for a June 15th opening date and well within budget: a testimony to the excellent work of local contractors Hickman's.

We hope that as many people as possible will be there on June 15th. We have engaged award-winning actress Coral White to declare the pool open and there'll be drinks and snacks available at the pool side. There'll also be a competition for the public to <u>decide</u> *Q14* <u>on the sculpture we plan to have at the entrance: you will decide which famous historical figure from the city we should have</u>.

And now, moving on to the Central Park Playground, which we're pleased to announce has just won the Douglas Award for safety: the news came through only last week. The unique design is based on the concept of the Global Village, with the playground being divided into six areas showing different parts of the world – each with a representative feature. For example, there is a section on <u>Asia, and this is represented by rides and equipment in the</u> *Q15* <u>shape of snakes, orang-utans, tigers and so on – fauna native to the forests of the region</u>. Moving south to the Antarctic – we couldn't run to an ice rink I'm afraid but opted instead

for climbing blocks in the shape of mountains – I thought they could have had slides for the   *Q16*
glaciers but the designers did want to avoid being too literal! Then on to South America –
and here the theme is El Dorado – games replicating the search for mines full of precious   *Q17*
stones. And then moving up to North America, here there was considerable debate – I
know the contribution of cinema and jazz was considered but the designers finally opted   *Q18*
for rockets and the International Space Station. Eastwards to Europe then, and perhaps
the most traditional choice of all the areas: medieval castles and other fortifications. Then   *Q19*
last, but not least, moving south to Africa and a whole set of wonderful mosaics and trails   *Q20*
to represent the great rivers of this fascinating and varied continent.

Now, the opening date for our Global Playground is 10th July. And again we'd love to see
you there – so make a date and come and see this magnificent, original new amenity right
in the heart of the city.

SECTION 3

VICTOR:	Right, well, for our presentation shall I start with the early life of Thor Heyerdahl?	
OLIVIA:	Sure. Why don't you begin with describing the type of boy he was, especially his passion for collecting things.	*Q21 & 22*
VICTOR:	That's right, he had his own little museum. And I think it's unusual for children to develop their own values and not join in their parents' hobbies; I'm thinking of how Heyerdahl wouldn't go hunting with his dad, for example.	
OLIVIA:	Yeah, he preferred to learn about nature by listening to his mother read to him. And quite early on he knew he wanted to become an explorer when he grew up. That came from his camping trips he went on in Norway I think …	
VICTOR:	No, it was climbing that he spent his time on as a young man.	*Q21 & 22*
OLIVIA:	Oh, right … After university he married a classmate and together, they decided to experience living on a small island, to find out how harsh weather conditions shaped people's lifestyles.	*Q23 & 24* *Q23 & 24*
VICTOR:	As part of their preparation before they left home, they learnt basic survival skills like building a shelter. I guess they needed that knowledge in order to live wild in a remote location with few inhabitants, cut off by the sea, which is what they were aiming to do.	
OLIVIA:	An important part of your talk should be the radical theory Heyerdahl formed from examining mysterious ancient carvings that he happened to find on the island. I think you should finish with that.	
VICTOR:	OK.	

OLIVIA:	All right, Victor, so after your part I'll talk about Thor Heyerdahl's adult life, continuing from the theory he had about Polynesian migration. Up until that time of course, academics had believed that humans first migrated to the islands in Polynesia from Asia, in the west.	
VICTOR:	Yes, they thought that travel from the east was impossible, because of the huge, empty stretch of ocean that lies between the islands and the nearest inhabited land.	*Q25*
OLIVIA:	Yes, but Heyerdahl spent ages studying the cloud movements, ocean currents and wind patterns to find if it was actually possible. And another	

argument was that there was no tradition of large ship-building in the communities lying to the east of Polynesia. But Heyerdahl knew they made lots of coastal voyages in locally built canoes.

VICTOR: Yes, or sailing on rafts, as was shown by the long voyage that Heyerdahl did next. It was an incredibly risky journey to undertake – sometimes I wonder if he did that trip for private reasons, you know? To show others that he could have spectacular adventures. What do you think, Olivia?

OLIVIA: Well, <u>I think it was more a matter of simply trying out his idea, to see if migration from the east was possible</u>.   *Q26*

VICTOR: <u>Yes, that's probably it</u>. And the poor guy suffered a bit at that time because the war forced him to stop his work for some years …

OLIVIA: Yes. When he got started again and planned his epic voyage, do you think it was important to him that he achieve it before anyone else did?

VICTOR: Um, I haven't read anywhere that that was his motivation. <u>The most important factor seems to have been that he use only ancient techniques and local materials to build his raft</u>.   *Q27*

OLIVIA: Yes. I wonder how fast it went.

VICTOR: Well, it took them 97 days from South America to the Pacific Islands.

OLIVIA: Mm. And after that, Heyerdahl went to Easter Island, didn't he? We should mention the purpose of that trip. I think he sailed there in a boat made out of reeds.

VICTOR: No, that was later on in Egypt, Olivia.

OLIVIA: Oh, yes, that's right.

VICTOR: But what he wanted to do was <u>talk to the local people about their old stone carvings and then make one himself to learn more about the process</u>.   *Q28*

OLIVIA: I see. Well, what a great life. Even though many of his theories have been disproven, he certainly left a lasting impression on many disciplines, didn't he? <u>To my mind, he was the first person to establish what modern academics call practical archaeology. I mean, that they try to recreate something from the past today</u>, like he did with his raft trip. It's unfortunate that his ideas about where Polynesians originated from have been completely discredited.   *Q29*

VICTOR: Yes. Right, well, I'll prepare a PowerPoint slide at the end that acknowledges our sources. I mainly used *The Life and Work of Thor Heyerdahl* by William Oliver. I thought the research methods he used were very sound, <u>although I must say I found the overall tone somewhat old-fashioned. I think they need to do a new, revised edition</u>.   *Q30*

OLIVIA: Yeah, I agree. What about the subject matter – I found it really challenging!

VICTOR: Well, it's a complex issue …

OLIVIA: I thought the book had lots of good points. What did you think of …

SECTION 4

Well, I've been talking to managers in a number of businesses, and reading surveys about the future of management. And what I'm going to present in this seminar is a few ideas about how the activity is likely to change in the next ten years. It isn't a scientific, statistical analysis – just some ideas for us to discuss.

One area I want to mention is business markets, and I'm sure a really significant development will be <u>a major increase in competition, with companies from all round the world trying to sell similar products</u>. Consumers will have much more choice – for instance, food products sold in Australia might be manufactured in the USA, China, Finland and dozens of other countries. At the same time, mergers and takeovers mean that <u>governments are actually losing power to major global corporations</u>. We can probably all think of companies that exert a great deal of influence, which may be good for consumers. A third point I want to make about markets is that <u>in the rapidly expanding economies, such as India, China, Brazil and Russia, demand is growing very fast</u>. This is putting pressure on resources all over the world.

Q31

Q32

Q33

I think businesses are becoming more open to external influences. In particular, <u>companies are consulting customers more and more before making their business decisions</u>. Companies are finding out what they want and providing it, instead of making products and then trying to sell them, which is the model of years ago.

Q34

Another influence is that <u>concerns about the environment will force manufacturers to extend product lifecycles, to reduce the amount of pollution and waste. And in some cases, regulation will need to be strengthened</u>.

Q35

Many societies are much more fluid and democratic, and the structure of companies is changing to reflect that. <u>I think we're going to see a greater emphasis within companies on teams created with a specific project in mind</u>. And when they're completed, the teams will be disbanded and new ones formed.

Q36

More and more people see work as simply one part of their lifestyle, and not the most important one, and as the workforce is shrinking in some countries, businesses are having to compete for staff instead of being able to choose among a lot of applicants. <u>Typical examples that will attract and retain staff are traditional ones like flexible hours</u> and – something that has been made possible by advances in technology – remote working, with people based at their home, abroad, or almost anywhere they choose.

Q37

Management styles will almost certainly continue to change. Senior managers will require a lot more than the efficiency that they've always needed. <u>Above all they'll need great skills in leadership</u>, so that their organisation can initiate and respond to change in a fast-moving world, where they face lots of competing requirements and potential conflicts.

Q38

In most of the world, the senior managers of large businesses are mainly men in their fifties and sixties. <u>The predominant style of management will almost certainly become more consultative and collaborative, caused above all, by more women moving into senior management positions</u>.

Q39

Many of the changes are influenced by developments in the wider economy. The traditional emphasis of business was manufacturing, and of course the service sector is very important. But we shouldn't overlook the growing financial contribution of IP, that is, intellectual property. Some books and films generate enormous sums from the sale of related DVDs, music, games, clothes, and so on.

Another point I'd like to make is that although I've been talking about companies, one trend that they have to face is the move away from people working for the same employer for years. <u>Instead, more and more people are becoming self-employed</u>, to gain the freedom and control over their lives that they're unlikely to get from being employed.

Q40

OK, well that's all I want to say, so let's open it up for discussion.

TEST 3

SECTION 1

DIRECTOR:	Good morning. Welcome to the Early Learning Childcare Centre. How may I help you?
CAROL:	Hi. I spoke to you last week about enrolling my daughter for next year.
DIRECTOR:	Oh, yes. I'll just get some details from you. So, you're her mother?
CAROL:	That's right.
DIRECTOR:	And, can I have your name?
CAROL:	It's Carol, Carol <u>Smith</u>.
DIRECTOR:	And your daughter's name?
CAROL:	It's Kate.
DIRECTOR:	Now, we have several groups at the centre and we cater for children from three to five years old. How old is your daughter?
CAROL:	She's three now but she turns four next month.
DIRECTOR:	<u>I'll put four down because that's how old she'll be when she starts</u>.
CAROL:	Fine, she's so excited about her birthday and coming to the centre.
DIRECTOR:	That's good to hear. And what's your address?
CAROL:	It's <u>46 Wombat</u> Road, that's W-O-M-B-A-T. Woodside 4032.
DIRECTOR:	And what's the phone number?
CAROL:	Oh … it's … 3345 9865.
DIRECTOR:	So, have you decided on the days you'd like to bring your daughter here?
CAROL:	I'd prefer Monday and Wednesday if possible.
DIRECTOR:	Mmm. I'll check, Monday's fine, but I think the centre is already full for Wednesday. Erm. Yes. Sorry. It seems to be a very popular day. We can offer you a Thursday or a Friday as well.
CAROL:	Oh dear. <u>I suppose Thursday would be all right</u> because she has swimming on Friday.
DIRECTOR:	OK, got that. Because a lot of parents work, we do offer flexible start and finish times. We are open from 7:30 in the morning until 6 o'clock at night. What time would you like your daughter to start?
CAROL:	I need to get to work in the city by 9:00 so <u>I'll drop her off at 8:30</u>. You're pretty close to the city here so that should give me plenty of time to get there.
DIRECTOR:	That's fine. Now, we also need to decide which group she'll be in. We have two different groups and they're divided up according to age. There's the green group, which is for three- to four-year-olds. And then there's the red group which is for four- to five-year-olds.
CAROL:	She's quite mature for her age and she can already write her name and read a little.
DIRECTOR:	Well, <u>I'll put her in the red group</u> and we can always change her to the green one if there are any problems.
CAROL:	That sounds fine.
DIRECTOR:	OK. Let's move on to meals. We can provide breakfast, lunch and dinner. As she's finishing pretty early, she won't need dinner, will you give her breakfast before she comes?
CAROL:	Yes, <u>she'll only need lunch</u>.

Example (Q1) (Q2) (Q3) (Q4) (Q5) (Q6)

DIRECTOR:	Now, does she have any medical conditions we need to know about? Does she have asthma or any hearing problems for example?
CAROL:	No. But <u>she does need to wear glasses</u>.

Q7

DIRECTOR:	Oh, I'll make a note of that.
CAROL:	Yes, she's pretty good about wearing them, she can't see much without them.
DIRECTOR:	Right. OK. Now, I also need emergency contact details.
CAROL:	So what sort of information do you need?
DIRECTOR:	Just the name and number of a friend or family member we can contact in case we can't get hold of you at any time.
CAROL:	OK. That'd better be my sister … Jenny <u>Ball</u>. That's B-A-double L. Her phone number is 3346 7523.

Q8

DIRECTOR:	Great. So <u>she is the child's aunt</u>?

Q9

CAROL:	Yes, that's right.
DIRECTOR:	I'll make a note of that as well. Now, is there anything you'd like to ask?
CAROL:	What about payment? How much are the fees each term?
DIRECTOR:	Well, for two days and the hours you've chosen, that will be $450 altogether.
CAROL:	OK, and do I have to pay that now?
DIRECTOR:	No, we send out invoices once the children start at the centre. You can choose to pay at the end of each term or we do offer a slightly discounted rate <u>if you pay every month</u>.
CAROL:	<u>Oh, I'll do that then</u>. I find it easier to budget that way and I'm not used to the term dates just yet.

Q10

DIRECTOR:	Good, it makes it a lot simpler for us as well. Well, that's everything. Would you like me to show you around …?

SECTION 2

INTERVIEWER:	Today we're pleased to have on the show Alice Bussell from the Dolphin Conservation Trust. Tell us about the Trust, Alice.
ALICE:	Well, obviously its purpose is to protect dolphins in seas all around the world. It tries to raise people's awareness of the problems these marine creatures are suffering because of pollution and other threats. It started ten years ago and it's one of the fastest growing animal charities in the country – although it's still fairly small compared with the big players in animal protection. We are particularly proud of the work we do in education – last year we visited a huge number of schools in different parts of the country, going round to talk to children and young people aged from five to eighteen. In fact, about thirty-five per cent of our members are children. <u>The charity uses its money to support campaigns – for example, for changes in fishing policy and so forth</u>. It hopes soon to be able to employ its first full-time biologist – with dolphin expertise – to monitor populations. Of course, many people give their services on a voluntary basis and <u>we now have volunteers working in observation, office work and other things</u>.

Q11 & 12

Q11 & 12

I should also tell you about the award we won from the Charity Commission last year – for our work in education. Although it's not meant an enormous amount of money for us, <u>it has made our activities even more widely publicised and understood</u>. In the long term it may not bring in extra members but we're hoping it'll have this effect.

Q13

| INTERVIEWER: | Is it possible to see dolphins in UK waters? |
| ALICE: | Yes. In several locations. And we have a big project in the east part of Scotland. This has long been a haven for dolphins because it has very little shipping. However, that may be about to change soon because oil companies want to increase exploration there. We're campaigning against this because, although there'll be little pollution from oil, <u>exploration creates a lot of underwater noise</u>. It means the dolphins can't rest and socialise. |

Q14

This is how I became interested in dolphin conservation in the first place. I had never seen one and I hadn't been particularly interested in them at school. <u>Then I came across this story about a family of dolphins who had to leave their home in the Moray Firth because of the oil companies and about a child who campaigned to save them. I couldn't put the book down – I was hooked.</u>

Q15

| INTERVIEWER: | I'm sure our listeners will want to find out what they can do to help. You mentioned the 'Adopt a Dolphin' scheme. Can you tell us about that? |
| ALICE: | Of course! People can choose one of our dolphins to sponsor. They receive a picture of it and news updates. I'd like to tell you about four which are currently being adopted by our members: Moondancer, Echo, Kiwi and Samson. Unfortunately, <u>Echo is being rather elusive this year and hasn't yet been sighted by our observers</u> but we remain optimistic that he'll be out there soon. All the others have been out in force – Samson and Moondancer are often photographed together but it is <u>Kiwi who's our real 'character' as she seems to love coming up close for the cameras and we've captured her on film hundreds of times</u>. They all have their own personalities – Moondancer is very elegant and curves out and into the water very smoothly, whereas <u>Samson has a lot of energy – he's always leaping out of the water with great vigour</u>. You'd probably expect him to be the youngest – he's not quite – that's Kiwi – but <u>Samson's the latest of our dolphins to be chosen for the scheme</u>. Kiwi makes a lot of noise so we can often pick her out straightaway. Echo and Moondancer are noisy too, but <u>Moondancer's easy to find because she has a particularly large fin on her back, which makes her easy to identify</u>. So, yes, they're all very different… |

Q16

Q17

Q18

Q19

Q20

| INTERVIEWER: | Well, they sound a fascinating group … |

SECTION 3

MIA:	Hi, Rob. How's the course going?
ROB:	Oh, hi, Mia. Yeah, great. I can't believe the first term's nearly over.
MIA:	I saw your group's performance last night at the student theatre. It was good.
ROB:	Really? Yeah … but now we have to write a report on the whole thing, an in-depth analysis. I don't know where to start. Like, I have to write about the role I played, the doctor, how I developed the character.
MIA:	Well, what was your starting point?
ROB:	Er … my grandfather was a doctor before he retired, and I just based it on him.

MIA:	OK, but how? Did you talk to him about it?
ROB:	He must have all sorts of stories, but he never says much about his work, even now. He has a sort of authority though.
MIA:	So how did you manage to capture that?
ROB:	I'd … <u>I'd visualise what he must have been like in the past, when he was sitting in his consulting room listening to his patients.</u> *Q21*
MIA:	OK, so that's what you explain in your report.
ROB:	Right.
MIA:	Then there's the issue of atmosphere – so in the first scene we needed to know how boring life was in the doctor's village in the 1950s, so when the curtain went up on the first scene in the waiting room, there was that long silence before anyone spoke. <u>And then people kept saying the same thing over and over, like 'Cold, isn't it?'</u> *Q22*
ROB:	Yes, and everyone wore grey and brown, and just sat in a row.
MIA:	Yes, all those details of the production.
ROB:	And I have to analyse how I functioned in the group – what I found out about myself. I know I was so frustrated at times, when we couldn't agree.
MIA:	Yes. So did one person emerge as the leader?
ROB:	Sophia did. That was OK – <u>she helped us work out exactly what to do, for the production. And that made me feel better, I suppose.</u> *Q23*
MIA:	When you understood what needed doing?
ROB:	Yes. And Sophia did some research, too. That was useful in developing our approach.
MIA:	Like what?
ROB:	Well, <u>she found these articles from the 1950s about how relationships between children and their parents, or between the public and people like bank managers or the police were shifting</u>. *Q24*
MIA:	Interesting. And did you have any practical problems to overcome?
ROB:	Well, in the final rehearsal everything was going fine until the last scene – that's where the doctor's first patient appears on stage on his own.
MIA:	The one in the wheelchair?
ROB:	Yes, and he had this really long speech, with the stage all dark except for one spotlight – <u>and then that stuck somehow so it was shining on the wrong side of the stage</u> … but anyway we got that fixed, thank goodness. *Q25*
MIA:	Yes, it was fine on the night.

ROB:	But while you're here, Mia, I wanted to ask you about the year abroad option. Would you recommend doing that?
MIA:	Yes, definitely. It's a fantastic chance to study in another country for a year.
ROB:	I think I'd like to do it, but it looks very competitive – there's only a limited number of places.
MIA:	Yes, so <u>next year when you are in the second year of the course, you need to work really hard in all your theatre studies modules. Only students with good marks get places – you have to prove that you know your subject really well.</u> *Q26*
ROB:	Right. So how did you choose where to go?
MIA:	<u>Well, I decided I wanted a programme that would fit in with what I wanted to do after I graduate, so I looked for a university with emphasis on acting rather than directing for example. It depends on you.</u> Then about six months before you go, you have to email the scheme coordinator with *Q27*

your top three choices. <u>I had a friend who missed the deadline and didn't</u>   *Q28*
<u>get her first choice, so you do need to get a move on at that stage.</u> You'll
find that certain places are very popular with everyone.

ROB: And don't you have to write a personal statement at that stage?

MIA: Yes.

ROB: Right. <u>I'll get some of the final year students to give me some tips</u> …   *Q29*
maybe see if I can read what they wrote.

MIA: I think that's a very good idea. I don't mind showing you what I did.
<u>And while you're abroad don't make the mistake I made. I got so involved</u>   *Q30*
<u>I forgot all about making arrangements for when I came back here for</u>
<u>the final year. Make sure you stay in touch so they know your choices for</u>
<u>the optional modules.</u> You don't want to miss out doing your preferred
specialisms.

ROB: Right.

SECTION 4

Today, I want to talk about self-regulatory focus theory and how the actions of leaders
can affect the way followers approach different situations. Self-regulatory focus theory is
a theory developed by Tori Higgins. He says that a person's focus at any given time is to
either approach pleasure or avoid pain. These are two basic motivations that each and
every one of us has, and they cause us to have different kinds of goals. <u>Promotion goals in</u>
<u>different life situations emphasise achievement</u>. Prevention goals are oriented towards the   *Q31*
avoidance of punishment.

In a specific situation, our thoughts might focus more on promotion goals or more on
prevention goals. The theory suggests that two factors affect which goals we are focusing
on. First, there is a chronic factor. <u>This factor is connected to a person's personality</u> and   *Q32*
says that each person has a basic tendency to either focus more on promotion goals
or focus more on prevention goals as part of his or her personality. <u>Second, there is a</u>
<u>situational factor which means that the context we are in can make us more likely to</u>   *Q33*
<u>focus on one set of goals or the other</u>. For example, <u>we are more likely to be thinking</u>
<u>about pleasure and to have promotion goals when we are spending time with a friend</u>. In   *Q34*
contrast, if we are working on an important project for our boss, we are more likely to try to
avoid making mistakes and therefore have more prevention goals in our mind.

Research has shown that the goals we are focusing on at a given time affect the way we
think. For example, <u>when focusing on promotion goals, people consider their ideal self,</u>
<u>their aspirations and gains</u>. They don't think about what they can lose, so they think in a   *Q35*
happier mode. They feel more inspired to change.

When people are focusing on prevention goals, they think about their "ought" self. What
are they supposed to be? What are people expecting from them? They consider their
obligations to others. As a result, they experience more anxiety and try to avoid situations
where they could lose.

Now that I have talked about the two focuses and how they affect people, I want to look
at the idea that <u>the way leaders behave, or their style of leading, can affect the focus</u>   *Q36*
<u>that followers adopt in a specific situation</u>. In talking about leadership, we often mention
transformational leaders and transactional leaders. <u>Transformational leaders, when</u>
<u>interacting with their followers, focus on their development</u>. In their words and actions   *Q37*

transformational leaders highlight change. Their speech is passionate and conveys a definitive <u>vision</u>. All of these things can encourage followers to think about what could be. In other words, they inspire a promotion focus in their followers. *Q38*

In contrast, <u>transactional leaders focus on developing clear structures that tell their followers exactly what is expected of them</u>. While they do explain the rewards people will get for following orders, they emphasise more how a follower will be punished or that a follower won't get rewarded if his or her behaviour doesn't change. In short, they emphasise the consequences of making a mistake. This emphasis will clearly lead followers to focus on avoiding punishment and problems. This is clearly a prevention focus. *Q39*

In conclusion, it is important to understand that one focus is not necessarily better than the other one. For a designer who works in a field where a lot of <u>innovation</u> is needed, a promotion focus is probably better. In contrast, a prevention focus which causes people to work more cautiously and produce higher quality work might be very appropriate for a job like a surgeon, for example. The main point of the research, though, is that the actions of leaders can greatly influence whether people approach a situation with more of a promotion focus or more of a prevention focus. *Q40*

TEST 4

SECTION 1

MR THORNDYKE:	Thorndyke's.
EDITH:	Good morning. Is that Mr Thorndyke?
MR THORNDYKE:	Speaking. How can I help?
EDITH:	I've got quite a few things which need painting and fixing in the flat and I wonder whether you'd be able to do the work.
MR THORNDYKE:	I'm sure I'd be able to help but let me take down a few details.
EDITH:	Yes, of course.
MR THORNDYKE:	Well, firstly, how did you hear about us?
EDITH:	<u>It was my friend May Hampton</u> … you did some excellent work for her a couple of years ago. Do you remember? *Example*
MR THORNDYKE:	Oh, yes, that was in West Park Flats, lovely lady.
EDITH:	Yes, she is.
MR THORNDYKE:	And what's your name, please?
EDITH:	It's Edith <u>Pargetter</u>. *Q1*
MR THORNDYKE:	Edith … can you spell your surname, please?
EDITH:	It's P-A-R-G-E-double T-E-R.
MR THORNDYKE:	Double T, right. And do you live in West Park Flats as well?
EDITH:	No, actually it's <u>East</u> Park, Flat 4. *Q2*
MR THORNDYKE:	Oh, right, that's over the road, I seem to remember – quite difficult to get to.
EDITH:	Yes, it's <u>at the back of the library</u>. *Q3*
MR THORNDYKE:	Right, I know. And what's your phone number?
EDITH:	875934 but I'm out a great deal in the afternoons and evenings.
MR THORNDYKE:	<u>So would the best time to ring you be in the morning?</u> *Q4*
EDITH:	Yes.

MR THORNDYKE:	Fine. I've made a note of that. Can I just ask, I'll be in a van and I know parking's rather difficult round your flats. Where would you recommend?	
EDITH:	Well, I always tell people in larger vehicles to <u>park by the postbox on the other side of the road from the entrance</u>.	Q5
MR THORNDYKE:	Good, thanks.	
EDITH:	And will you be able to give me a full itemised quote?	
MR THORNDYKE:	Oh, yes, <u>I'll list all the jobs separately with individual prices.</u>	Q6
EDITH:	That'd be a great help.	
MR THORNDYKE:	No problem.	

MR THORNDYKE:	Now, what would you like me to do?	
EDITH:	Firstly and most urgently is in the kitchen. With all the weather damage, <u>the glass in the door has cracked and I'd need that fixing …</u>	
MR THORNDYKE:	<u>I presume you mean replacing?</u>	Q7
EDITH:	Oh, yes. And as soon as possible …	
MR THORNDYKE:	What I'll do is come round tomorrow morning and do that immediately.	
EDITH:	Thank you so much. The other things aren't so urgent but …	
MR THORNDYKE:	Now, I'll make a note of everything you want doing.	
EDITH:	Well, in the kitchen I'd like some painting doing.	
MR THORNDYKE:	All the kitchen walls?	
EDITH:	<u>Just the area over the cooker</u>. It's very greasy …	Q8
MR THORNDYKE:	Right … it does tend to get that way!	
EDITH:	Yes!	
MR THORNDYKE:	Well, if you want a proper job done what I'd need to do is <u>strip the old paint and plaster it about a week before I paint it.</u>	Q9
EDITH:	Of course. Now, May tells me you also do work in the garden.	
MR THORNDYKE:	That's right.	
EDITH:	Well, I'd like you to <u>replace a fence</u>.	Q10
MR THORNDYKE:	Just one?	
EDITH:	Yes, at the far end.	
MR THORNDYKE:	Fine. Shouldn't be a problem.	
EDITH:	And that's the lot.	
MR THORNDYKE:	Fine. Yeah, as I say I can come round tomorrow morning to look over things with you.	
EDITH:	That's great, thank you.	
MR THORNDYKE:	So, I'll look forward to seeing you tomorrow at …	

SECTION 2

Welcome to Manham Port, where a thousand years of history are brought to life. All the family can enjoy a day out at Manham: visit our copper mine, see models of the machinery it used, have your photo taken in nineteenth-century costume, experience at first hand how people lived at different stages throughout history, and especially how children studied, worked and played.

The port of Manham is located in beautiful and peaceful countryside, on a bend in the great River Avon, <u>and developed here because it's the highest navigable point of the Avon – boats can go no higher up this river – and proved a handy place to load and unload cargo to and from the sea</u>, which is over 23 miles away. A small port was already   Q11

established here when, about 900 years ago, tin was discovered nearby, <u>though it wasn't</u>   *Q12*
<u>until the Industrial Revolution, when a tremendous need for metals of all kinds developed,</u>
<u>that Manham expanded to become one of the busiest ports in the country</u>. And because
it was already so busy, prospectors began to look for other minerals, and by the end of
the nineteenth century, lead, copper, manganese and arsenic were added to the cargos
leaving Manham.

In the early days, the ores had been smelted – or processed – in the same area they were
mined. But, as demand grew, the smelting process required huge factory furnaces or fires
to melt the metal from the rock and <u>there was not enough coal in the local area, so the</u>   *Q13*
<u>rocks containing minerals had to be shipped long distances</u>.

Sadly, <u>in the twentieth century, the great port of Manham declined, and thousands of</u>   *Q14*
<u>workers were forced to emigrate out of the area</u>. The building at the port fell into disrepair,
and the place became almost forgotten. But then, the Manham Trust was formed to
conserve the historical resources of the area. It organised scores of local volunteers to
remove undergrowth to find the original outlines of the installations. <u>It then brought in paid</u>   *Q15*
<u>professionals to match installations with maps of the original port complex and to set about</u>
<u>reconstructing it.</u> Today you can see the results of this ambitious programme of restoration.
The intention, and we believe this will be realised before the end of the year, is to return
Manham Port to the condition it reached at its peak as 'the greatest copper port in the
country'.

But what can you do and see on your visit today? Here are just a few highlights. We
suggest you start with the visit to the copper mine. <u>Travel on converted mining trains and</u>   *Q16*
<u>journey into the depths of the mountain along seams once worked by hundreds of miners</u>.
Watch out especially for the great pumping machines which rid the mine of water. But
please be warned that, <u>like all mines, ours is very dark and closed in and we do say that</u>   *Q17*
<u>children under five and also dogs should NOT be taken into the mine</u>.

The next recommended visit is to the village school. <u>While looking round the classrooms,</u>   *Q18*
<u>take a special look at our display of games, which is one of the largest in the world</u>. And <u>it's</u>   *Q19*
<u>recommended that you time your visit to coincide with a guided tour</u>. This will give you the
opportunity to ask lots of questions. Near the school is the beautiful old sailing ketch called
'The George'. You are welcome to board the boat and look round the cabins. Look out for
the ship's wheel which was missing until only five years ago when it was dredged out of
the silt by a local fisherman. We have no idea how it got there but it's been polished and
proudly restored to its original place on the boat. <u>Please take care going down the ladders</u>   *Q20*
<u>if you wish to visit the lower deck – we don't recommend you allow young children to use</u>
<u>them</u>.

So we hope you have a memorable visit to Manham Port and will tell your friends all
about us.

SECTION 3

TIM:	Hi, Laura – could you spare a few minutes to talk about the work placement you did last summer? I'm thinking of doing one myself …
LAURA:	Hi, Tim. Sure.
TIM:	Didn't you do yours at an environmental services company?
LAURA:	That's right … It's only a very small company and they needed

	someone to produce a company brochure, and I wanted to get some business experience because I'm interested in a career in occupational psychology in a business environment. It was good because I had overall responsibility for the project.
TIM:	What kind of skills do you think you developed on the placement? I mean, apart from the ones you already had … Did you have to do all the artwork for the brochure, the layout and everything?
LAURA:	We hired the services of a professional photographer for that. I did have to use my IT skills to a certain extent because I cut and pasted text from marketing leaflets, but that didn't involve anything I hadn't done before.
TIM:	Do you think you got any better at managing your time and prioritising things? You always used to say you had trouble with that …
LAURA:	Oh, definitely. There was so much pressure to meet the project deadline. And I also got better at explaining things and asserting my opinions, because I had to have weekly consultations with the marketing manager and give him a progress report.
TIM:	It sounds as if you got a lot out of it then.
LAURA:	Absolutely. It was really worthwhile … But you know, the company benefited too …
TIM:	Yes, they must have done. After all, if they'd used a professional advertising agency to produce their brochure instead of doing it in-house, presumably they'd have paid a lot more?
LAURA:	Oh, yes. I worked it out – it would have been 250 per cent more. And I thought the end result was good, even though we did everything on site. The company has quite a powerful computer and I managed to borrow some scanning software from the university. The new brochure looks really professional; it enhances the image of the company straight away.
TIM:	So in the long run it should help them to attract clients, and improve their sales figures?
LAURA:	That's the idea. Yeah.

Q21 & 22 (TIM) / Q21 & 22 (LAURA) / Q23 & 24 (LAURA)

TIM:	Well, all in all it sounds very positive – I think I will go ahead and apply for a placement myself. How do I go about it?
LAURA:	It's easy enough to do, because there's a government agency called STEP – S-T-E-P – that organises placements for students. You should start by getting their booklet with all the details – I expect you can download one from their website.
TIM:	Actually, they've got copies in the psychology department – I've seen them there. I'll just go to the office and pick one up.
LAURA:	Right. And then if I were you, after I'd looked at it I'd go over all the options with someone …
TIM:	I suppose I should ask my tutor's advice. He knows more about me than anyone.
LAURA:	One of the career officers would be better, they've got more knowledge about the jobs market than your personal tutor would have.
TIM:	OK …
LAURA:	And then when you know what you want you can register with STEP – you'll find their address in the booklet. And once you've registered they assign you to a mentor who looks after your application.
TIM:	And then I suppose you just sit back and wait till you hear something?
LAURA:	They told me at the careers office that it's best to be proactive, and get

Q25 (TIM) / Q26 (LAURA) / Q27 (LAURA)

148

updates yourself by checking the website for new placement alerts. Your mentor is supposed to keep you informed, but you can't rely on that.

TIM: I don't suppose it's a good idea to get in touch with companies directly, is it?

LAURA: Not really … But it is the company who notifies you if they want you to go   Q28
for an interview. You get a letter of invitation or an email from personnel departments.

TIM: And do I reply directly to them?

LAURA: Yes, you do. STEP only gets involved again once you've been made a job offer.

TIM: Right … So, once you've had an interview you should let your mentor   Q29
know what the outcome is? I mean whether you're offered a job, and whether you've decided to accept it?

LAURA: That's right. They'll inform the careers office once a placement has been agreed, so you don't have to do that.

TIM: Is that all then?

LAURA: More or less. Only once you've accepted an offer you'll probably have to supply a reference, because the placement will be conditional on that. And that's something you should ask your own tutor to provide. He knows   Q30
about your academic ability and also about your qualities, like reliability.

TIM: Well, thanks very much for the information – I'm starting to look forward …

SECTION 4

Today we're going to look at an important area of science, namely nanotechnology. So what is it? Nano means tiny, so it's science and engineering on the scale of atoms and molecules. The idea is that by controlling and rearranging atoms, you can literally create anything. However, as we'll see, the science of the small has some big implications affecting us in many ways.

There's no doubt that nanotechnology promises so much for civilisation. However, all new technologies have their teething problems. And with nanotechnology, society often gets the   Q31
wrong idea about its capabilities. Numerous science-fiction books and movies have raised people's fears about nanotechnology – with scenarios such as inserting little nano-robots into your body that monitor everything you do without you realising it, or self-replicating nano-robots that eventually take over the world.

So how do we safeguard such a potentially powerful technology? Some scientists   Q32
recommend that nano-particles be treated as new chemicals with separate safety tests and clear labelling. They believe that greater care should also be taken with nano-particles in laboratories and factories. Others have called for a withdrawal of new nano products such as cosmetics and a temporary halt to many kinds of nanotech research.

But as far as I'm concerned there's a need to plough ahead with the discoveries and   Q33
applications of nanotechnology. I really believe that most scientists would welcome a way to guard against unethical uses of such technology. We can't go around thinking that all innovation is bad, all advancement is bad. As with the debate about any new technology, it is how you use it that's important. So let's look at some of its possible uses.

Thanks to nanotechnology, there could be a major breakthrough in the field of transportation with the production of more durable metals. These could be virtually unbreakable, lighter and much more pliable leading to planes that are 50 times lighter than at present. Those same improved capabilities will dramatically reduce the cost of travelling into space making it more accessible to ordinary people and opening up a totally new holiday destination.

Q34
Q35

In terms of technology, the computer industry will be able to shrink computer parts down to minute sizes. We need nanotechnology in order to create a new generation of computers that will work even faster and will have a million times more memory but will be about the size of a sugar cube. Nanotechnology could also revolutionise the way that we generate power. The cost of solar cells will be drastically reduced so harnessing this energy will be far more economical than at present.

Q36
Q37

But nanotechnology has much wider applications than this and could have an enormous impact on our environment. For instance, tiny airborne nano-robots could be programmed to actually rebuild the ozone layer, which could lessen the impact of global warming on our planet. That's a pretty amazing thought, isn't it? On a more local scale, this new technology could help with the clean-up of environmental disasters as nanotechnology will allow us to remove oil and other contaminants from the water far more effectively. And, if nanotechnology progresses as expected – as a sort of building block set of about 90 atoms – then you could build anything you wanted from the bottom up. In terms of production, this means that you only use what you need and so there wouldn't be any waste.

Q38
Q39

The notion that you could create anything at all has major implications for our health. It means that we'll eventually be able to replicate anything. This would have a phenomenal effect on our society. In time it could even lead to the eradication of famine through the introduction of machines that produce food to feed the hungry.

But it's in the area of medicine that nanotechnology may have its biggest impact. How we detect disease will change as tiny biosensors are developed to analyse tests in minutes rather than days. There's even speculation nano-robots could be used to slow the ageing process, lengthening life expectancy.

Q40

As you can see, I'm very excited by the implications that could be available to us in the next few decades. Just how long it'll take, I honestly don't know.

Listening and Reading Answer Keys

TEST 1

LISTENING

Section 1, Questions 1–10

1. Ardleigh
2. newspaper
3. theme
4. tent
5. castle
6. beach/beaches
7. 2020
8. flight
9. 429
10. dinner

Section 2, Questions 11–20

11&12 IN EITHER ORDER
- A
- C

13. health problems
14. safety rules
15. plan
16. joining
17. free entry
18. peak
19. guests
20. photo card / photo cards

Section 3, Questions 21–30

21. C
22. A
23. B
24. A
25. C
26. presentation
27. model
28. material/materials
29. grant
30. technical

Section 4, Questions 31–40

31. gene
32. power/powers
33. strangers
34. erosion
35. islands
36. roads
37. fishing
38. reproduction
39. method/methods
40. expansion

If you score…

0–11	12–26	27–40
you are unlikely to get an acceptable score under examination conditions and we recommend that you spend a lot of time improving your English before you take IELTS.	you may get an acceptable score under examination conditions but we recommend that you think about having more practice or lessons before you take IELTS.	you are likely to get an acceptable score under examination conditions but remember that different institutions will find different scores acceptable.

ACADEMIC READING

Reading Passage 1, Questions 1–13

1	FALSE
2	TRUE
3	NOT GIVEN
4	NOT GIVEN
5	TRUE
6	pavilions
7	drought
8	tourists
9	earthquake
10	4/four sides
11	tank
12	verandas/verandahs
13	underwater

Reading Passage 2, Questions 14–26

14	viii
15	iii
16	xi
17	i
18	v
19	x
20	ii
21	iv
22	TRUE
23	FALSE
24	NOT GIVEN
25	NOT GIVEN
26	FALSE

Reading Passage 3, Questions 27–40

27	C
28	A
29	D
30	B
31	G
32	E
33	A
34	F
35	B
36	NO
37	YES
38	NOT GIVEN
39	NOT GIVEN
40	NO

If you score…

0–11	12–27	28–40
you are unlikely to get an acceptable score under examination conditions and we recommend that you spend a lot of time improving your English before you take IELTS.	you may get an acceptable score under examination conditions but we recommend that you think about having more practice or lessons before you take IELTS.	you are likely to get an acceptable score under examination conditions but remember that different institutions will find different scores acceptable.

TEST 2

LISTENING

Section 1, Questions 1–10

1   Hardie
2   19
3   GT8 2LC
4   hairdresser
5   dentist/dentist's
6   lighting
7   trains
8   safe
9   shower
10   training

Section 2, Questions 11–20

11   A
12   C
13   C
14   A
15   E
16   F
17   D
18   H
19   A
20   B

Section 3, Questions 21–30

21&22   *IN EITHER ORDER*
     B
     C
23&24   *IN EITHER ORDER*
     B
     E
25   A
26   C
27   C
28   A
29   B
30   A

Section 4, Questions 31–40

31   competition
32   global
33   demand
34   customers
35   regulation
36   project
37   flexible
38   leadership
39   women
40   self-employed

If you score…

0–11	12–28	29–40
you are unlikely to get an acceptable score under examination conditions and we recommend that you spend a lot of time improving your English before you take IELTS.	you may get an acceptable score under examination conditions but we recommend that you think about having more practice or lessons before you take IELTS.	you are likely to get an acceptable score under examination conditions but remember that different institutions will find different scores acceptable.

ACADEMIC READING

Reading Passage 1, Questions 1–13

1	iv
2	viii
3	vii
4	i
5	vi
6	ix
7	ii
8	NOT GIVEN
9	TRUE
10	FALSE
11	FALSE
12	NOT GIVEN
13	TRUE

Reading Passage 2, Questions 14–26

14	A
15	D
16	F
17	D
18	B
19	D
20	E
21	A
22	C
23	*IN EITHER ORDER; BOTH REQUIRED FOR ONE MARK* books (and) activities
24	internal regulation / self-regulation
25	emotional awareness
26	spoon-feeding

Reading Passage 3, Questions 27–40

27	B
28	H
29	L
30	G
31	D
32	C
33	D
34	A
35	D
36	NOT GIVEN
37	NO
38	YES
39	NOT GIVEN
40	NO

If you score...

0–12	13–28	29–40
you are unlikely to get an acceptable score under examination conditions and we recommend that you spend a lot of time improving your English before you take IELTS.	you may get an acceptable score under examination conditions but we recommend that you think about having more practice or lessons before you take IELTS.	you are likely to get an acceptable score under examination conditions but remember that different institutions will find different scores acceptable.

TEST 3

LISTENING

Section 1, Questions 1–10

1	4
2	46 Wombat
3	Thursday
4	8.30
5	red
6	lunch
7	glasses
8	BALL
9	aunt
10	month

Section 2, Questions 11–20

11&12	**IN EITHER ORDER**
	C
	E
13	B
14	A
15	C
16	B
17	C
18	D
19	D
20	A

Section 3, Questions 21–30

21	C
22	A
23	A
24	B
25	B
26	E
27	D
28	A
29	G
30	C

Section 4, Questions 31–40

31	achievement / achievements
32	personality / character
33	Situational
34	friend
35	aspirations / ambitions
36	style
37	development
38	vision
39	structures
40	innovation / innovations

If you score…

0–11	12–27	28–40
you are unlikely to get an acceptable score under examination conditions and we recommend that you spend a lot of time improving your English before you take IELTS.	you may get an acceptable score under examination conditions but we recommend that you think about having more practice or lessons before you take IELTS.	you are likely to get an acceptable score under examination conditions but remember that different institutions will find different scores acceptable.

ACADEMIC READING

Reading Passage 1, Questions 1–13

1 ii
2 i
3 v
4 vii
5 TRUE
6 NOT GIVEN
7 NOT GIVEN
8 TRUE
9 NOT GIVEN
10 FALSE
11 source of income / industry
12 employer
13 domestic tourism

Reading Passage 2, Questions 14–26

14 C
15 B
16 H
17 B
18 E
19 sun(light)
20 upper
21 dry
22 north
23 FALSE
24 TRUE
25 NOT GIVEN
26 B

Reading Passage 3, Questions 27–40

27 B
28 F
29 I
30 G
31 D
32 C
33 A
34 D
35 C
36 NO
37 YES
38 NOT GIVEN
39 YES
40 NOT GIVEN

If you score...

0–11	12–27	28–40
you are unlikely to get an acceptable score under examination conditions and we recommend that you spend a lot of time improving your English before you take IELTS.	you may get an acceptable score under examination conditions but we recommend that you think about having more practice or lessons before you take IELTS.	you are likely to get an acceptable score under examination conditions but remember that different institutions will find different scores acceptable.

TEST 4

LISTENING

Section 1, Questions 1–10

1 Pargetter
2 East
3 library
4 morning/mornings
5 postbox
6 prices
7 glass
8 cooker
9 week
10 fence

Section 2, Questions 11–20

11 B
12 B
13 A
14 A
15 C
16 trains
17 dark
18 games
19 guided tour
20 ladder/ladders

Section 3, Questions 21–30

21&22 *IN EITHER ORDER*
   A
   E
23&24 *IN EITHER ORDER*
   B
   C
25 D
26 F
27 G
28 B
29 E
30 C

Section 4, Questions 31–40

31 C
32 B
33 C
34 metal/metals
35 space
36 memory
37 solar
38 oil
39 waste
40 tests

If you score...

0–11	12–27	28–40
you are unlikely to get an acceptable score under examination conditions and we recommend that you spend a lot of time improving your English before you take IELTS.	you may get an acceptable score under examination conditions but we recommend that you think about having more practice or lessons before you take IELTS.	you are likely to get an acceptable score under examination conditions but remember that different institutions will find different scores acceptable.

ACADEMIC READING

Reading Passage 1, Questions 1–13

1 spread
2 10/ten times
3 below
4 fuel
5 seasons
6 homes/housing
7 TRUE
8 FALSE
9 TRUE
10 TRUE
11 NOT GIVEN
12 FALSE
13 FALSE

Reading Passage 2, Questions 14–26

14 transformation/change
15 young age
16 optimism
17 skills/techniques
18 negative emotions / feelings
19 E
20 C
21 G
22 A
23 E
24 C
25 G
26 H

Reading Passage 3, Questions 27–40

27 C
28 D
29 C
30 B
31 A
32 F
33 G
34 A
35 B
36 D
37 NOT GIVEN
38 YES
39 NO
40 YES

If you score...

0–11	12–28	29–40
you are unlikely to get an acceptable score under examination conditions and we recommend that you spend a lot of time improving your English before you take IELTS.	you may get an acceptable score under examination conditions but we recommend that you think about having more practice or lessons before you take IELTS.	you are likely to get an acceptable score under examination conditions but remember that different institutions will find different scores acceptable.

GENERAL TRAINING TEST A

Section 1, Questions 1–14

1	TRUE
2	FALSE
3	NOT GIVEN
4	TRUE
5	FALSE
6	TRUE
7	NOT GIVEN
8	C
9	E
10	D
11	E
12	C
13	E
14	G

Section 2, Questions 15–27

15	decision maker
16	impact
17	opening
18	white envelope
19	brochure
20	(free) sample
21	response rate
22	(international) profile
23	publications
24	website content
25	audience
26	purpose
27	post-graduate

Section 3, Questions 28–40

28	E
29	A
30	A
31	B
32	E
33	F
34	A
35	B
36	D
37	E
38	I
39	G
40	B

If you score…

0–16	17–28	29–40
you are unlikely to get an acceptable score under examination conditions and we recommend that you spend a lot of time improving your English before you take IELTS.	you may get an acceptable score under examination conditions but we recommend that you think about having more practice or lessons before you take IELTS.	you are likely to get an acceptable score under examination conditions but remember that different institutions will find different scores acceptable.

GENERAL TRAINING TEST B

Section 1, Questions 1–14

1	FALSE
2	FALSE
3	TRUE
4	NOT GIVEN
5	NOT GIVEN
6	TRUE
7	FALSE
8	ii
9	x
10	v
11	iii
12	ix
13	vi
14	iv

Section 2, Questions 15–27

15	FALSE
16	FALSE
17	NOT GIVEN
18	TRUE
19	TRUE
20	FALSE
21	F
22	B
23	G
24	H
25	C
26	G
27	D

Section 3, Questions 28–40

28	C
29	F
30	A
31	E
32	A
33	B
34	C
35	B
36	C
37	C
38	prepared mind
39	iodine vapour/vapor
40	chemical/chemicals

If you score…

0–18	19–30	31–40
you are unlikely to get an acceptable score under examination conditions and we recommend that you spend a lot of time improving your English before you take IELTS.	you may get an acceptable score under examination conditions but we recommend that you think about having more practice or lessons before you take IELTS.	you are likely to get an acceptable score under examination conditions but remember that different institutions will find different scores acceptable.

Model and sample answers for Writing tasks

TEST 1, WRITING TASK 1

SAMPLE ANSWER

This is an answer written by a candidate who achieved a **Band 4.5** score. Here is the examiner's comment:

> The response generally addresses the requirements of the task but there is no clear overview. Key features of the two pie charts are presented but not adequately covered, and there is a tendency to focus on details without referring to the bigger picture. Organisation is evident. The relationship of ideas can be followed (*and*, *First*, *but*, *Secondly*, *The former*, *The latter*) but the sentences are not fluently linked to each other. Vocabulary is limited but just adequate for the task. Simple vocabulary is used accurately but the range does not allow much variation in expression. There are noticeable errors in spelling, though these do not cause strain. A limited range of grammatical structures is used; subordinate clauses are rare and most sentences are simple. Even simple sentences often contain errors (*The latter have*), so grammatical errors are frequent and can cause severe strain for the reader. Control over sentence formation is weak.

This chart shows the energy comsuption of an average Australian household and how propotion of emitting greenhouse gas in each type of active.

First, the most bigger different informations are using heating and other appliances, relate to 42% and 15%, but they going up side down in gas emittions, which is 15% and 28%.

Secondly, using energy of lighting and refrigeration are similar change in greenhouse gas emittions. The former using 4% energy and produce double number of emittions to 8%. The latter have the same situation about 7% in using energy but emit 14% greenhouse gas.

The last two parts of things are water heating which is second large source of using energy and the smallest cumsuming energy one = cooling. Indeed, there are just a marginally change in greenhouse gas emittions which grow from 30% to 32% and rise from 2% to 3%.

TEST 1, WRITING TASK 2

MODEL ANSWER

This model has been prepared by an examiner as an example of a very good answer. However, please note that this is just one example out of many possible approaches.

One important stage in a child's growth is certainly the development of a conscience, which is linked to the ability to tell right from wrong. This skill comes with time and good parenting, and my firm conviction is that punishment does not have much of a role to play in this. Therefore I have to disagree almost entirely with the given statement.

To some extent the question depends on the age of the child. To punish a very young child is both wrong and foolish, as an infant will not understand what is happening or why he or she is being punished. Once the age of reason is reached however, a child can be rewarded for good behaviour and discouraged from bad. This kind but firm approach will achieve more than harsh punishments, which might entail many negative consequences unintended by the parents.

To help a child learn the difference between right and wrong, teachers and parents should firstly provide good role modelling in their own behaviour. After that, if sanctions are needed, the punishment should not be of a physical nature, as that merely sends the message that it is acceptable for larger people to hit smaller ones – an outcome which may well result in the child starting to bully others. Nor should the punishment be in any way cruel.

Rather, teachers and parents can use a variety of methods to discipline their young charges, such as detention, withdrawal of privileges, and time-out. Making the punishment fit the crime is a useful notion, which would see children being made to pick up rubbish they have dropped, clean up graffiti they have drawn, or apologise to someone they have hurt. In these ways responsibility is developed in the child, which leads to much better future behaviour than does punishment.

TEST 2, WRITING TASK 1

MODEL ANSWER

This model has been prepared by an examiner as an example of a very good answer. However, please note that this is just one example out of many possible approaches.

> The two tables contain sales data for Fairtrade coffee and bananas in 1999 and 2004, in five nations of Europe.
>
> The first table shows low-level coffee sales increasing in all five countries, albeit to widely varying degrees. In two places sales increased by the same small amount: 1.8–2 million euros in Denmark, and 0.8–1 million in Sweden. The increment was slightly larger in Belgium, from 1–1.7 million euros. Meanwhile, in Switzerland sales doubled from 3–6 million euros. Finally, in the UK there was an enormous increase, from 1.5–20 million euros.
>
> In the second table, it is Switzerland which stands out as buying far more Fairtrade bananas than the other four countries. Swiss sales figures jumped from 15–47 million euros across these five years, while in the UK and Belgium sales only grew from 1–5.5 and from 0.6–4 million euros respectively. Sweden and Denmark showed a different pattern, with falls in banana sales from 1.8–1 and 2–0.9 million euros.
>
> Comparing the two tables, it is clear that in 1999 Fairtrade coffee sales ranged from 0.8–3 million euros in these five countries, while banana sales also mostly clustered between 0.6 and 2 million euros, with Switzerland the outlier at a huge 15 million euros. By 2004, sales figures for both products had risen across the board, except for Sweden and Demark which recorded drops in banana sales.

Model and sample answers for Writing tasks

TEST 2, WRITING TASK 2

SAMPLE ANSWER

This is an answer written by a candidate who achieved a **Band 3.5** score. Here is the examiner's comment:

> This response is too short at only 232 original words, so does not meet the minimum length required for the task. It is difficult to work out what the writer is trying to say, as his/her position is not made clear. The ideas do seem to be relevant, but problems in the writing mean that no part of the task is adequately addressed. Although some linking words and phrases are used, and the paragraphing looks helpful on the page, the order of information is not coherent and the response does not progress clearly to the end. The vocabulary is basic and the writer has only limited control of word formation. The spelling errors cause strain for the reader. Two lengthy phrases have been copied from the writing question paper. Some complex grammatical structures are attempted but are all faulty. Some simple structures are correct but overall errors predominate. Commas, fullstops and capital letters are misused throughout so punctuation is faulty.

All of us,agree that all University students have maind can They use to think and choose a way life. The goverments need to be better in the future.

The big quistion? How can we fuind the answer fo relaize interested students and the goverments?

First of all. who the some people think that all university students should study whatever they like. There are experts. The experts could be give us the result suitable for the students, and drew for Them the good choose. also, should be The goverment put plan for future. for example, How many pailot, How many teatcher or tuter the country need. Moreover, In schools, help students for choose what they like of job. Furthermore, coumet all the Minstor togather. (togather much better)

on the other hand, I think not good idea a drew the way for students. such as, take who funsh study in school to study soubject we like Not what he like. and thes same as me. when I was student, me tuter told me "please studey computer science", and my do not like computer science. Now, I will study another subject. I have aim and I can do what I like. I agree with people. who siad only be allowed to study subjects that will be useful in the future.

in conclusion, I would like to say that the students have maind. They with our recommend to them. They will be live one of the good lives in countries also the science and technology plays rule importent in our life.

I hop you

TEST 3, WRITING TASK 1

SAMPLE ANSWER

This is an answer written by a candidate who achieved a **Band 6.5** score. Here is the examiner's comment:

> This response reports the data on the bar charts accurately and gives an extended overview at the end. Information is logically organised and there is a clear progression throughout. The message can be followed with ease as a range of cohesive devices are used flexibly. Referencing and substitution are also well managed, however there are lapses in paragraphing. A range of vocabulary is used with no spelling errors, though word choice is not always appropriate (*to seek further study*, *roughly almost*, *the percentage on the amount of*, overuse of *sought*). These errors do not detract from overall clarity but they do reduce the communicative effect. A range of complex structures is also used accurately. Error-free sentences are frequent and only a few mistakes occur (*The graphs represents*, *we will notice*), so grammar and punctuation are generally well controlled.

The graphs represents what UK graduates and postgraduates did after leaving college in 2008.

On the first graph, it shows that 17,735 graduate students sought part-time employment in 2008 while 3,500 did voluntary work and 29,665 decided to seek further study. According to the graph, 16,235 graduate students were unemployed after college, which is roughly almost the same amount as those who sought part-time work.

On the second graph, we see that 2,535 UK postgraduates did part-time work while only 345 did voluntary work. 2,725 UK postgraduates decided to study further which is slightly more than those who decided to take part-time employment. Lastly, 1,625 UK postgraduate students were not in the work force. The overall trend shows that most of the students, graduates and postgraduates alike, sought out further education while only a small number of students in both groups did voluntary work after leaving college. We will also notice that about a third in each group were unemployed. Lastly, the only difference that we will notice between the two groups is the percentage on the amount of students who went on to do part-time work with only one-third of the total amount in the graduate students and almost one-half with the postgraduate students.

TEST 3, WRITING TASK 2

MODEL ANSWER

This model has been prepared by an examiner as an example of a very good answer. However, please note that this is just one example out of many possible approaches.

It is said that countries are becoming similar to each other because of the global spread of the same products, which are now available for purchase almost anywhere. I strongly believe that this modern development is largely detrimental to culture and traditions worldwide.

A country's history, language and ethos are all inextricably bound up in its manufactured artefacts. If the relentless advance of international brands into every corner of the world continues, these bland packages might one day completely oust the traditional objects of a nation, which would be a loss of richness and diversity in the world, as well as the sad disappearance of the manifestations of a place's character. What would a Japanese tea ceremony be without its specially crafted teapot, or a Fijian kava ritual without its bowl made from a certain type of tree bark?

Let us not forget either that traditional products, whether these be medicines, cosmetics, toys, clothes, utensils or food, provide employment for local people. The spread of multinational products can often bring in its wake a loss of jobs, as people turn to buying the new brand, perhaps thinking it more glamorous than the one they are used to. This eventually puts old-school craftspeople out of work.

Finally, tourism numbers may also be affected, as travellers become disillusioned with finding every place just the same as the one they visited previously. To see the same products in shops the world over is boring, and does not impel visitors to open their wallets in the same way that trinkets or souvenirs unique to the particular area do.

Some may argue that all people are entitled to have access to the same products, but I say that local objects suit local conditions best, and that faceless uniformity worldwide is an unwelcome and dreary prospect.

TEST 4, WRITING TASK 1

MODEL ANSWER

This model has been prepared by an examiner as an example of a very good answer. However, please note that this is just one example out of many possible approaches.

Salmon begin life as eggs on a pebbly riverbed, hidden among reeds in the slow-moving upper reaches of a river. After five to six months the eggs hatch into 'fry'. For approximately the next four years, these baby salmon will live in the lower, faster-flowing waters of their river. During this time they measure between three and eight centimetres in length.

By the time salmon reach twelve to fifteen centimetres, they are termed 'smolt', and at this time they migrate further downriver into the open sea. After five years at sea the salmon will have grown to adult size, which is between seventy and seventy-six centimetres. They then begin swimming back to their birthplace, where they will lay their eggs, and the cycle starts anew.

In summary, the salmon passes through three distinct physical stages as it grows to maturity. Each of these stages takes place in a very different aquatic location. It is noteworthy that the first two stages of this fish's life occur in a freshwater environment, while the third stage is lived in saltwater.

TEST 4, WRITING TASK 2

SAMPLE ANSWER

This is an answer written by a candidate who achieved a **Band 5.5** score. Here is the examiner's comment:

> This script is too short at only 219 words, so fails to meet the minimum word count required by the task. However it does address all parts of the prompt, and presents a relevant position. The main ideas are clear and developed but could be more fully extended and supported. Information is arranged coherently and there is a clear overall progression, with adequate use of linking words (*However*, *also*, *Usually*, *since*, *but*, *So*) and paragraphing. The vocabulary is generally adequate and appropriate for the task (*funds*, *maintain*) and meaning is generally clear. However, misuse of the word *admission* and other slight inappropriacies (*doing a charity*) show a lack of precision in word choice. Many different complex structures are used but there are still fairly frequent errors. However, these rarely impede communication; in general grammar and punctuation are fairly well controlled.

Museums are unique places where you get to experience the history from past to the latest technology. However admission is required when entering.

Museums are popular places to go to on a weekends with family or friends. Admissions are one of the funds which keeps the museum running and also to maintain its exibits. Without admission museums would be dirty, pourly maintained, and likely impossible to operate, unless funded from goverment or charity.

However admissions are one thing which may keep the customer from entering. Usually we have to pay around $30 for admissions. Children or family which doesn't earn much simply can not afford such amount. They will go to museum which is free or even not go and experience the greatness of the museum, which I think is horrible because it should be open for everyone.

I think having an admission is a disadvantage since museums should be open for everyone, but admissions are essential for running the museums. So I think it is very important to come up with a plan so that museums could be operated but also be admission free, such as goverment funding or doing a charity. Auckland Museum is one great example. It is one of the biggest museums in New Zealand but it is also free of admission since it's goverment funded.

TEST A, WRITING TASK 1 (GENERAL TRAINING)

MODEL ANSWER

This model has been prepared by an examiner as an example of a very good answer. However, please note that this is just one example out of many possible approaches.

Dear Sally,

My departure date for New Zealand is drawing near, and I am busy with preparations. I have enrolled at an institution called 'ABC English' in Wellington, for a six-month Advanced course, full-time. It is quite expensive but I am hopeful of improving my pronunciation, especially.

To assist in covering the costs of my study, I aim to find a part-time job. Not only are the college fees rather high, but also I know that rental accommodation in the capital city will not be cheap, to say nothing of food and heating expenses! So I would very much like to arrange some temporary employment before I arrive.

I was wondering if you could ask around among your friends and colleagues to see if anyone wants a house-cleaner, gardener, or nanny for their children. I know you have a wide social network in Wellington which you could canvas for me, if you wouldn't mind. I'd be so grateful.

I look forward to seeing you soon.

Best wishes,

Margot

TEST A, WRITING TASK 2 (GENERAL TRAINING)

SAMPLE ANSWER

This is an answer written by a candidate who achieved a **Band 5** score. Here is the examiner's comment:

> Both parts of the prompt are addressed, although the main ideas and the writer's position could be better developed. No clear conclusions are drawn so there is a lack of overall progression. Organisation is evident but not always logical, and the sentences are not fluently linked to each other, while each paragraph lacks a clear topic. The vocabulary is limited but minimally adequate, with not much variation in expression, and the frequent spelling errors are noticeable and cause some difficulty for the reader. The range of sentence types is limited and rather repetitive. Complex sentences are attempted but tend to be faulty, and there are a number of basic errors. Punctuation is poorly controlled, with underuse of capital letters and fullstops.

I am going to write obout how the amount of crime is increasing in many countries and why.

Nowdays there are many countries has increasing on the amount of crime and I think the problem is that most of the crim has done by the young people which is under 18 and from the age you can see and you can understand what is going on but in my openion I think the main causes is the family and the school, the family I mean the mum an dad they have to look after theire tenagers until they grow up and do not let them watch films which has a fight or blod, the school is the same as the second house for the tenagers and they have to teach them how to grow up in good way and teach them how to respect the old people.

For example I have been told from my oldest brother that in the UK 2 years ago a boy from Qatar he is 16 years old has killed by groube of tenagers in Haisting and they killed him without any reasons and when the Police asked them why did you do that they said we want to show of we are the best. So you can say they learn from the action movies.

Finaly I hope all the people can help the tenagers to give them advice and to let them know what will happen after the crime. Also in schools they must teach them how to avoied the bad movies and to grow up in safe way.

TEST B, WRITING TASK 1 (GENERAL TRAINING)

SAMPLE ANSWER

This is an answer written by a candidate who achieved a **Band 8** score. Here is the examiner's comment:

> The response addresses all the bullet points very naturally, and expands fully on two of them. The reason for the celebration is covered at the beginning and the end, but could be more fully developed. The message is easy to follow, ideas are logically sequenced and all aspects of cohesion are well managed. The paragraphing is sufficient but could be improved: the three short, single-sentence paragraphs would be better combined into one. A wide range of vocabulary is fluently used to convey precise meanings. There are several spelling errors which do not reduce the communicative effect. A wide range of grammatical structures is accurately used, with full flexibility and control. Punctuation and grammar are appropriate throughout, with no errors.

Dear Sir or Madam,

I am writing to you to express my delight with the excellent service and high quality of food that your restaurant provided us last Saturday night, on the occassion of my 50th birthday.

We were a party of twelve, which included my family, close friends and collegues from work. Your staff went out of their way to provide seating arrangements that were easily accessible, and did not interfere with other diners. I find that this is unusual in many restaurants these days. The waiters were extremely professional and polite, and were obviously experienced as they did not encroach too much on the procedings.

Your current menu offers a great deal of choice, as does your wine list, and everything was available. There were no complaints about the quality or quantity of the dishes served, and the presentation of each dish was akin to the dishes produced in shows such as 'Master Chef'.

I ordered the rack of pork ribs, which was deliciously succulent and, if anything, maybe slightly too large. Nevertheless, I managed to finish it!

I was similarly impressed with the large variety of local and International wines available. The wine that was ordered arrived at the correct temperature that each wine should be consumed at. The waiters were familiar with the etiquette of drinking and enjoying fine wines; and the service was paramount.

All-in-all, our group enjoyed a delicious meal at your establishment, and I had a very happy birthday.

Congratulations once again.

Yours sncerely

TEST B, WRITING TASK 2 (GENERAL TRAINING)

MODEL ANSWER

This model has been prepared by an examiner as an example of a very good answer. However, please note that this is just one example out of many possible approaches.

It is true that many parents purchase a multitude of playthings for their offspring. Whether or not this is a good thing for the child, is a moot point. On the face of it the advantages seem most apparent, but could there be a downside to this phenomenon of devoted parenting as well?

Most people would consider children who have many toys to be the fortunate ones. Interesting things to play with stimulate many positives in the young boy or girl, such as optimum brain development, hand-eye coordination and colour recognition, apart from the simple joy of playing. Modern toys are designed to be educational as well as fun, and concerned parents carefully select products which might speed their child's acquisition of numbers or the alphabet.

Is it possible that owning multiple toys could be in any way detrimental to a child? This is an unusual question, but there are some hidden pitfalls. For one, wealthy parents might spoil their son or daughter by showering him/her with toys, resulting in a negative effect on the child's character. For another, a growing child's concentration span may suffer if they are constantly surrounded by too many tempting objects, so that they become unable to focus on any one game for a decent length of time before being distracted. On the social side, older children may become targets of envy from classmates, if they are perceived as having far more possessions than their peers. Finally, the majority of toys today are made of plastic which commonly contains the chemical BPA, proven to be dangerous for infants to suck on or ingest.

It is clear then that this situation is not as straightforward as it first appears. It would seem that one of the many duties of parents is to make an informed choice about how many toys they buy for their young ones.

Sample answer sheets

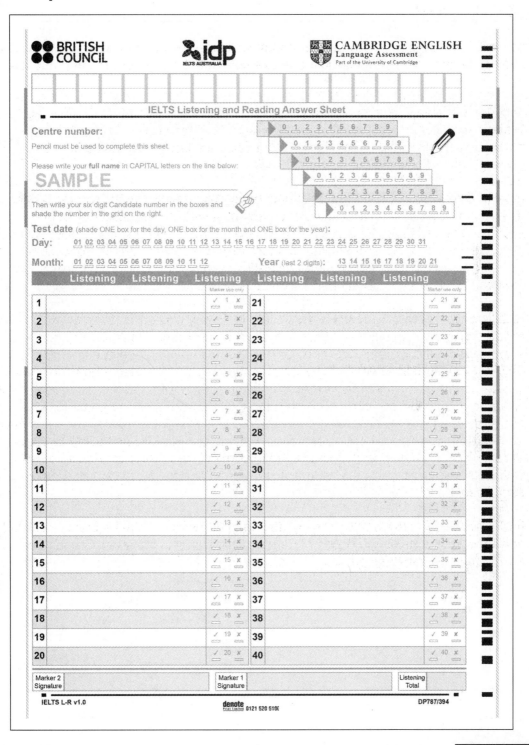

Sample answer sheets

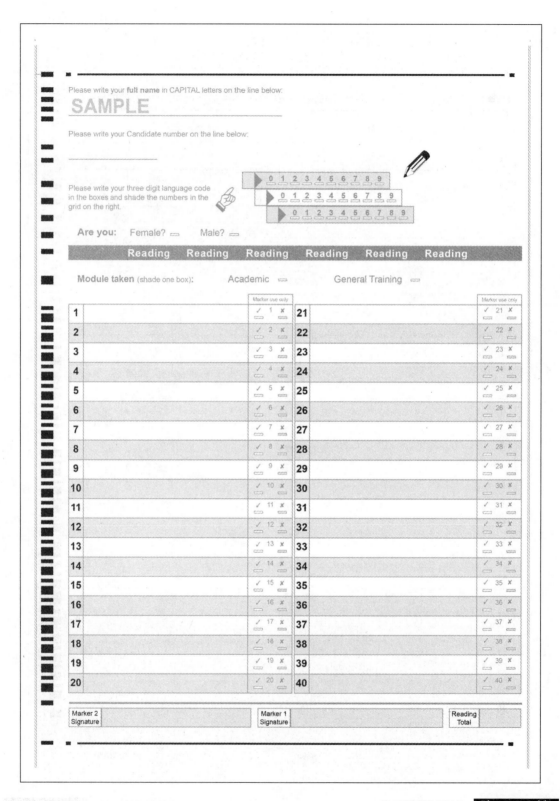

Please write your **full name** in CAPITAL letters on the line below:

SAMPLE

Please write your Candidate number on the line below:

Please write your three digit language code in the boxes and shade the numbers in the grid on the right.

0 1 2 3 4 5 6 7 8 9
0 1 2 3 4 5 6 7 8 9
0 1 2 3 4 5 6 7 8 9

Are you: Female? ▭ Male? ▭

Reading   Reading   Reading   Reading   Reading   Reading

Module taken (shade one box): Academic ▭   General Training ▭

		Marker use only				Marker use only
1		✓ 1 ✗	21			✓ 21 ✗
2		✓ 2 ✗	22			✓ 22 ✗
3		✓ 3 ✗	23			✓ 23 ✗
4		✓ 4 ✗	24			✓ 24 ✗
5		✓ 5 ✗	25			✓ 25 ✗
6		✓ 6 ✗	26			✓ 26 ✗
7		✓ 7 ✗	27			✓ 27 ✗
8		✓ 8 ✗	28			✓ 28 ✗
9		✓ 9 ✗	29			✓ 29 ✗
10		✓ 10 ✗	30			✓ 30 ✗
11		✓ 11 ✗	31			✓ 31 ✗
12		✓ 12 ✗	32			✓ 32 ✗
13		✓ 13 ✗	33			✓ 33 ✗
14		✓ 14 ✗	34			✓ 34 ✗
15		✓ 15 ✗	35			✓ 35 ✗
16		✓ 16 ✗	36			✓ 36 ✗
17		✓ 17 ✗	37			✓ 37 ✗
18		✓ 18 ✗	38			✓ 38 ✗
19		✓ 19 ✗	39			✓ 39 ✗
20		✓ 20 ✗	40			✓ 40 ✗

Marker 2 Signature	Marker 1 Signature	Reading Total

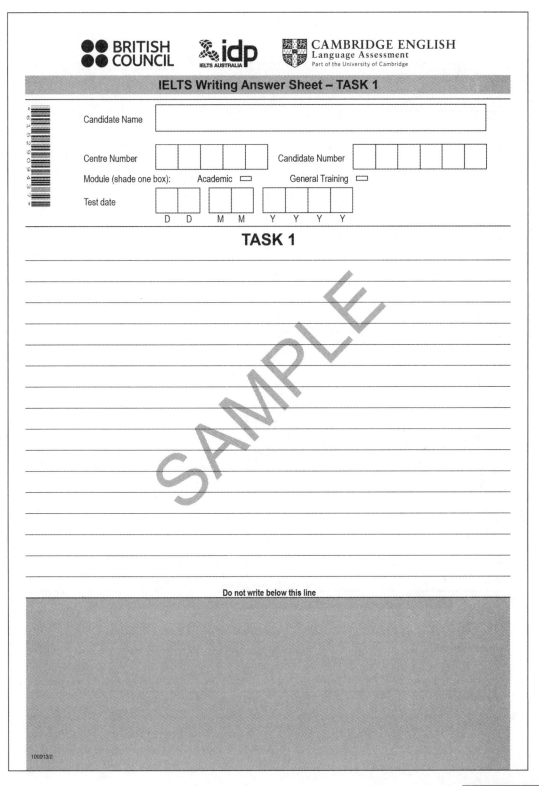

BRITISH COUNCIL

idp IELTS AUSTRALIA

CAMBRIDGE ENGLISH
Language Assessment
Part of the University of Cambridge

IELTS Writing Answer Sheet – TASK 1

Candidate Name

Centre Number

Candidate Number

Module (shade one box):   Academic ☐   General Training ☐

Test date

D D   M M   Y Y Y Y

TASK 1

Do not write below this line

100913/2

Sample answer sheets

[lined answer space]

SAMPLE

Do not write below this line

OFFICIAL USE ONLY

Candidate Number:								TA		CC		LR		GRA	

Examiner 2 Number:							

Underlength	No. of words	Penalty		Off-topic	Memorised	Illegible

Candidate Number:								TA		CC		LR		GRA	

Examiner 1 Number:							

Underlength	No. of words	Penalty		Off-topic	Memorised	Illegible

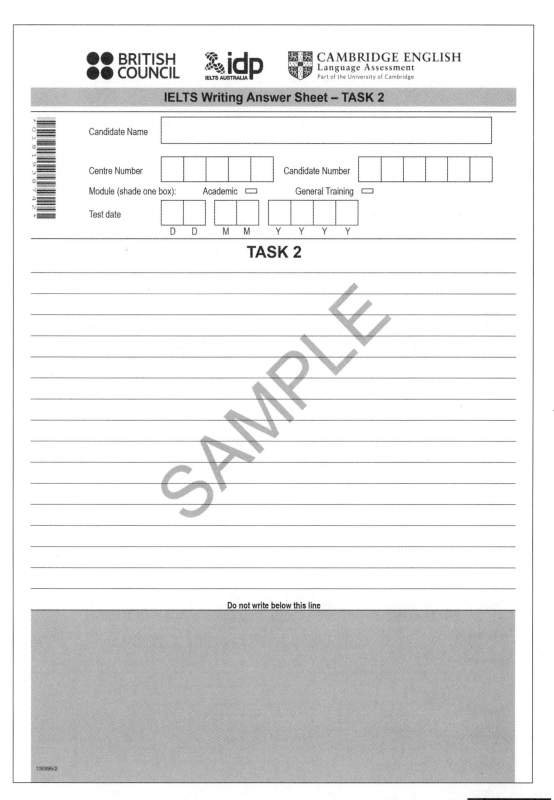

IELTS Writing Answer Sheet – TASK 2

Candidate Name

Centre Number

Candidate Number

Module (shade one box): Academic ☐   General Training ☐

Test date

D D M M Y Y Y Y

TASK 2

Do not write below this line

100895/2

© UCLES 2015   Photocopiable

Sample answer sheets

SAMPLE

Do not write below this line

OFFICIAL USE ONLY

Candidate Number:							TR		CC		LR		GRA	

| Examiner 2 Number: | | | | | | |

Underlength	No. of words	Penalty		Off-topic	Memorised	Illegible

Candidate Number:							TR		CC		LR		GRA	

| Examiner 1 Number: | | | | | | |

Underlength	No. of words	Penalty		Off-topic	Memorised	Illegible

Acknowledgements

The authors and publishers acknowledge the following sources of copyright material and are grateful for the permissions granted. While every effort has been made, it has not always been possible to identify the sources of all the material used, or to trace all copyright holders. If any omissions are brought to our notice, we will be happy to include the appropriate acknowledgements on reprinting.

Design Council and Haymarket Media for the text on pp. 25–26 adapted from 'The Psychology of Innovation' by Paul Simpson, *Design Council Magazine,* Summer 2007. Reproduced with permission; The Ian Sommerhalder Foundation for the text on p. 16 adapted from 'The Spirit Bear'. Reproduced with permission; Royal Geographical Society for the text on pp. 17–18 adapted from 'Stepwells' by Richard Cox, *Geographical,* Feb. 2008. Reproduced with permission; European Union for the text on pp. 22–23 from 'European Transport policy for 2010: time to decide' by the Commission of the European Communities, 12.9.2011. http://eur-lex.europa.eu, © European Union, 1998–2014; Charted Management Institute for the text on pp. 25–26 adapted from 'Looking Forward to a Decade of Change' by Sue Mann, *Professional Manager,* May 2008. Reproduced with permission; Rory Gear for the text on pp. 38, 137–138 from 'The Kon Tiki Man.' Reproduced with permission; Alcohol in Moderation for the text on pp. 42–43 adapted from 'Did Tea and Beer Make Britain Great?', *AIM Digest.* Reproduced with permission; Joan Freeman for the text on pp. 45–46 from 'Gifted Lives: What Happens When Gifted Children Grow Up.' Reproduced with permission; Palgrave Macmillan for extract on pp. 49–50 from *Readings in Popular Culture* edited by Gary Day, published 1990 Palgrave Macmillan reproduced with permission of Palgrave Macmillan; Dr. William Theobald for the text on pp. 65–66 from *Global Tourism.* Reproduced with permission; Penguin Canada Books for the extract on pp. 68–69 from *The Velocity of Honey: and More Science of Everyday Life* by Jay Ingham. Copyright © 2003, 2006. Used with permissions of Penguin Group (Canada); National Geographic Society for the text on pp. 72–74 from 'Beyond the Blue Horizon,' *National Geographic,* March 2008. Reproduced with permission; The Christian Science Publishing Society for excerpt on pp. 88–89 from 'Wildfire policy: Time for US to rely less on shovels, hoses, retardant?' by Daniel B. Wood, *Christian Science Monitor,* 5.6.2013. Copyright © The Christian Science Monitor; Text on pp. 92–93 adapted from 'Second Nature' by Kathleen McGowan, *Psychology Today,* 31.3.2008; Reed Business Information for the text on pp. 97–98 adapted from 'The Ancestor within All Creatures' by Michael Le Page, *News Scientist,* 15.1.2007. © Reed Business Information–UK. All rights reserved. Distributed by Tribune Content Agency; Text on p. 104 adapted from 'Fire Safety and Prevention: Smoke Alarms in the Home' by NSW Fire Brigades; Gordon Ell for extract on pp. 112–113 from *Kauri Gum and the Gumdiggers* by Dr. Bruce W. Hayward, published by Gordon Ell, The Bush Press, Auckland, NZ 1989; Flying Fish UK for the text on p. 121 adapted from 'A Successful Gap Year.' With permission; John Wiley & Sons for extract on pp. 125–126 from *Accidental Discoveries in Science* by Royston M. Roberts. Copyright © 1989 Wiley Science Editions; Duke University Fuqua School of Business for audio and script on pp. 62, 144 adapted from 'New Directions in Leadership Research' New Directions in Leadership Research Conference 31.5.2008. Copyright © 2014 Duke University.

Photo acknowledgements

The authors and publishers acknowledge the following sources of copyright material and are grateful for the permissions granted. While every effort has been made, it has not always been possible to identify the sources of all the material used, or to trace all copyright holders. If any omissions are brought to our notice, we will be happy to include the appropriate acknowledgements on reprinting.

Test 2 Reading Passage 3: © The Gallery Collection/Corbis; General Training Reading and Writing Test A Section 1: © Chimpinski/Shutterstock; General Training Reading and Writing Test A Section 3: © Wyco/iStock/Getty; General Training Reading and Writing Test B Section 2: © lestyan/Shutterstock.